THE ULTIMATE UNOFFICIAL
GUIDE TO ROBLOXING

THE ULTIMATE UNOFFICIAL
GUIDE TO ROBLOXING

EVERYTHING YOU NEED TO KNOW TO BUILD AWESOME GAMES!

CHRISTINA MAJASKI

Sky Pony Press
New York

Sky Pony Press books may be purchased in bulk at special discounts for sales promotion, corporate gifts, fund-raising, or educational purposes. Special editions can also be created to specifications. For details, contact the Special Sales Department, Sky Pony Press, 307 West 36th Street, 11th Floor, New York, NY 10018 or info@ skyhorsepublishing.com.

Sky Pony® is a registered trademark of Skyhorse Publishing, Inc.®, a Delaware corporation.

Visit our website at www.skyponypress.com.
Authors, books, and more at SkyPonyPressBlog.com.

10 9 8 7 6 5 4 3 2 1

Library of Congress Cataloging-in-Publication Data is available on file.

Cover design by Brian Peterson
Cover and interior photographs by Christina Majaski

Print ISBN: 978-1-5107-3087-8
eISBN: 978-1-5107-3096-0

Printed in China

TABLE OF CONTENTS

CHAPTER 1

What in the World Is Roblox?

The world of online gaming changes quickly, with new games popping up all the time. While you might be familiar with popular games like Minecraft, Angry Birds, and Sims, Roblox is likely a little bit newer to you. Whether you're a hardcore gamer who is always on top of the latest games, a newbie to the world of Roblox, or a parent or guardian trying to find out what in the world this is, we're here for you. In this guide, we will cover everything you need to know about Roblox (as well as some things you probably don't need to know), and by the end you'll be a Roblox pro.

Welcome to Roblox!

builderman
Mar 20, 2017 | 4:34 PM

Hello, and welcome to Roblox! My name is Builderman. I started Roblox so you and your friends can experience just about anything you could possibly imagine across millions of immersive user-generated 3D worlds, whether you're sailing across the open seas, exploring the farthest reaches of outer space, or hanging out with your friends in a virtual club. I'm here to make sure your experience stays fun, safe, and creative.

Before you jump in and start playing, here's a few tips. You can **customize your avatar** using our massive catalog of clothing and accessory options. Once you're set, pick something to play by checking out **our most popular games!** Did you know you can also play games with your friends across different devices at the same time, even if you're on a computer and they're using their phone or VR headset? **Finding friends on Roblox** is easy! Visit our forums, join or create a group, or invite others to play a game with you by sending them a chat message. Last but not least, be sure to read more about our rules and our account safety tips **here**.

That's all there is to it! Now, get ready for an epic adventure. We hope you have a blast!

Sincerely,

Builderman, CEO of Roblox

WHAT IS ROBLOX? A SHORT EXPLANATION

You might find when you first enter the world of Roblox that it's much more complicated than it looks. At the same time, it's also easier to get the hang of than

you might initially think. Roblox, in simplest terms, is a user-generated online social gaming platform where players create virtual worlds and can design their own games.

What is Roblox?

Roblox helps power the imagination of people around the world. As the world's largest social platform for play, over 48 million players come to Roblox every month to create adventures, play games, roleplay, and learn with friends. We call it the "Imagination Platform" and believe everyone should have the right to play on it. That is why Roblox is freely available on all modern smartphones, tablets, desktops, Xbox One, Oculus Rift, and HTC Vive.

Keep reading ⌄

Although part of the fun of Roblox is the ability to create your own worlds and games, many people especially enjoy the opportunity to explore 3D worlds. Roblox games allow you to explore, craft, and create items, gather resources, and engage in combat. You can build and develop games through the application called Roblox Studio, which comes free with the game.

Roblox can currently be played on nearly any kind of device or platform, including PC, Mac, iOS, Android, Oculus, and Xbox. You can pretty much play the game on any device – we'll help you get started with each device in later chapters.

In addition, you can customize your character with a wide variety of head shapes, body shapes, clothing, hats, and other types of gear. You can also create your own articles of clothing if you don't find your particular style already available. If you also want to sell the clothing you design, you will need to become a member of Builders Club, which is a premium Roblox club that includes extra privileges. However, even without

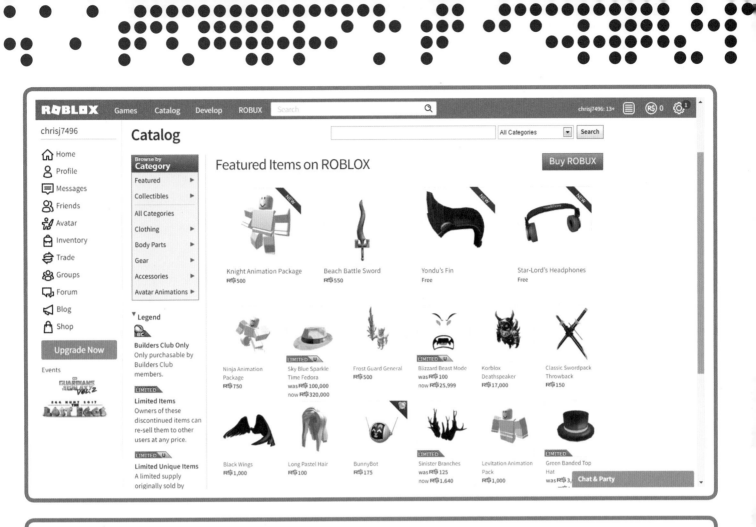

Builders Club you have the option of creating T-shirts, which are decals that you can attach to the front of a torso. Roblox also gives you the option of collecting and trading items, which can be an excellent opportunity to change up your style from time to time without costing you anything – especially if you have limited-edition collector's items.

THE HISTORY OF ROBLOX

Sometimes getting an understanding of the history of a game can help you master it a little more quickly. Although to some Roblox might seem like a fairly new game, it was originally created by founder David Baszucki and co-founder Erik Cassel way back in 2004, and released and published by Roblox Corporation in 2006. You might not have realized it, but the name Roblox is a combination of the words "robots" and "blocks," which kind of sums up what this game entails.

In February 2013, Erik Cassel died after battling cancer for three years. Later that year the Developer's Exchange, or DevEx, was released, allowing users to exchange Robux, the Roblox currency, for U.S. dollars. In order to become part of DevEx, the requirements are that you have at least 100,000 Robux, are a member of the Outrageous Builders Club, and have a valid PayPal account. The current trade ratio is approximately 500 Robux to one dollar. By September 2016, Roblox had paid out $7 million to community developers.

As of 2016, there were more than half a million game creators creating games, with more than 30 million active players per month, logging more than 300 million hours of game play. Today, the corporation employs hundreds of people in its California headquarters.

You might be interested in Roblox's charitable efforts as well. These include donations of a portion of its sales to causes such as relief for victims of the Haiti earthquake as well as research to find cures for cancer and amyotrophic lateral sclerosis (ALS), also known as Lou Gehrig's disease. In 2011, the sale of nearly 24,000 in-game hats on Roblox generated more than $10,000 for the Tohoku earthquake and tsunami in only two days.

Before you get started with Roblox, you might want to share some information with your parents. One of the features Roblox players enjoy is the social interaction – you can add other people you meet in the game as your friends while you're playing. An update to the game replaced the Friends and Best Friends system with Friends and Followers so that you can add up to 200 friends and an infinite number of followers. You can also join community groups and then advertise a group, participate in group relations, or set your primary group.

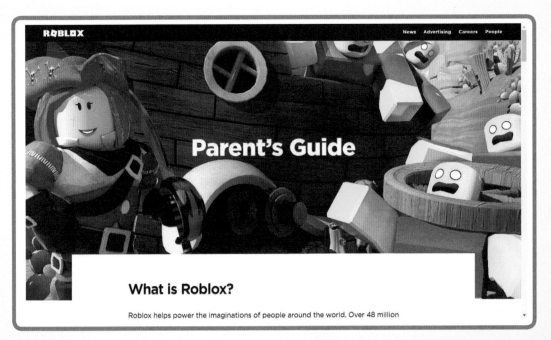

While there have been concerns surrounding the ability to connect with others on Roblox, you and your parents should know that Roblox takes safety seriously. Roblox provides a safe, moderated place to meet, play, create, and collaborate with others, and is widely considered to be an educational game for learning constructionism, designing, and building.

The platform, according to Roblox, is a family-friendly environment where kids' safety and privacy is very important. First, the game is compliant with the Children's Online Privacy Protection Act (COPPA), which addresses the privacy concerns of users who are age 12 and under. This measure means that these gamers are prevented from sharing personal information through chat messages or other in-game methods. Users who are 13 years of age or older can expand the vocabulary list in the settings, but Roblox's moderation team uses a

filtering system to make sure players are safe and not sharing personal information.

Recently, Roblox has added features to help with child-safety initiatives, which include

parental controls so that chat can be turned off, age visibility so parents can ensure the settings are age-appropriate, and more stringent chat controls for players under 13 years of age. The moderation team has also expanded in order to aggressively delete games and content that include inappropriate behavior. Any image, video, or audio files that you upload are pre-reviewed by the moderators to make sure the content is appropriate before it appears on the site.

On top of these measures, players can always report inappropriate chat messages or content through the Roblox Report Abuse system, which you can find throughout the site and while you're playing. You can also block anyone you want from chatting with you in-game or on the website.

Now that you've gotten a brief history of Roblox and have the basics under your belt, you're ready to get started. You'll be creating worlds, building, playing, and meeting other Roblox gamers like yourself in no time.

CHAPTER 3

Playing Roblox on Xbox One

Press Any Button To Begin

If you're getting ready to play Roblox on an Xbox One console, here's what you need to get started. You need not only an Xbox One but also an Xbox Gold account, as well as an Internet connection. You will find Roblox for free in the Xbox Live store.

You should first ask your parents' permission to change the settings if you're on a Family account. Otherwise, you can launch Roblox on Xbox One. You will see two buttons: one button allows you to play as your Gamertag and the other allows you to sign in to your Roblox account. Here you will sign in and then enter your Roblox account information on the next screen.

You can find the games you want to play on the Home screen and the Games screen. You can also find the games you've played in the Recently Played Games section of the Home screen. You can access the controller map whenever you need it in-game by clicking on Roblox Menu and selecting the Settings option. You will need to press up on the left thumbstick and click the Right Bumper to get to the Help tab. Of course, each game you play will likely have different rules, controls, and mechanics, but for the most part they'll be the same once you get used to them.

Currently, features like friends, chat, groups, and forums are unavailable on Xbox One, but you can access them from a PC, Mac, or mobile device. Builders Club is also not available, but you can buy and use Robux with Xbox One. To purchase Robux, you simply need to be logged in to your Xbox Live account.

You can also create games using Roblox Studio on a PC or Mac and then play them on your Xbox One console.

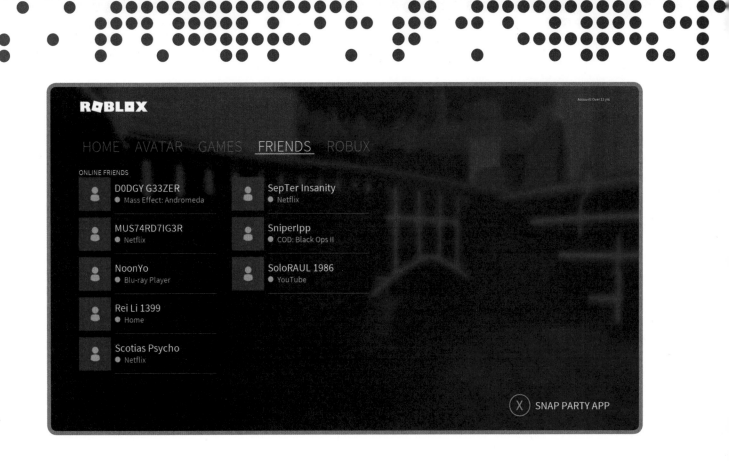

For avatar items, you will see the option to Get Robux, which takes you to the Robux page, where you can make your purchases. For in-game items, you will see a prompt with the lowest amount needed to buy the item. You'll also see the Robux screen on the main game screen, where you can buy Robux anytime you like. You can also buy Robux from the Xbox Live website, but if you buy Robux from the Roblox website or through mobile apps, you can't use them on Xbox, nor can you redeem Roblox Game Cards on Xbox.

You can use Robux you've purchased on Xbox One to buy new packages to change how your Roblox avatar looks. You can find these items on the Avatar screen when you select the Avatar image or by pressing the Right Bumper. You can also buy other perks, upgrades, and items inside the games for Xbox, but you'll see these displayed when you're inside, along with options and pricing according to the game.

CHANGING YOUR AVATAR

You can change your avatar on Roblox with Xbox by going to the Avatar tab and choosing whatever you like. You'll see a number of free avatars, as well as some you can buy with Robux. If you want to customize your avatar further you'll need to go to the Roblox website and log in using your Xbox Roblox account credentials. Here you can choose hats, hair, arms, legs, and anything else you want to change about your avatar on Xbox.

CHATTING ON XBOX ONE

If you want to chat with your friends and party members, there are many ways to chat on Roblox with Xbox One using its integrated voice chat system. In-game chat allows you to communicate if you have a microphone connected to a headset or Kinect. This automatically places you into voice chat with other players in the game. However, you must enable voice communication in your Xbox Settings for this to work. Xbox Live Party Chat is used to chat with Xbox Live friends, which overrides in-game chat when the feature is active. You can also switch to in-game chat through the Your Party panel in Xbox and selecting Switch to Game Chat.

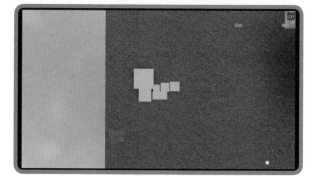

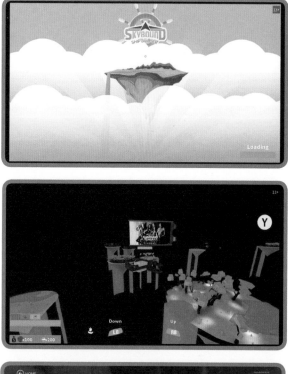

One of the newest and most exciting ways to play Roblox is with Oculus Rift. To do this, you will first need to install Roblox and then open the Oculus app on your computer. You can then select the gear icon at the top right and choose Gear Settings. After that, select General from the menu on the left, and then go to the Unknown Sources setting and make sure it appears as a check instead of an "x."

Comfort [edit]

ROBLOX as a platform is always working to do whatever it can on the engine and platform side to ensure a comfortable experience. This includes creating good default camera and movement controls, including comfort as a sort parameter, and removing core 2D GUI elements. But there are many things that you, as a developer, can do beyond the platform to provide a comfortable experience.

Movement [edit]

Camera motion can be a big contributor towards motion and simulator sickness. Some of the best experiences in VR involve little to no camera motion outside tracking the player's head motions. That said, if you do need the camera to move beyond head tracking, there are a few practices that you can follow to ensure a more comfortable experience.

Make sure any motion is slow and at a constant velocity. Accelerations in general can cause motion sickness. Keep in mind acceleration does not just mean acceleration forward. Falling, turning, swinging, all of these motions fundamentally involve acceleration. Jumping for instance can be quite uncomfortable in VR, even if it is explicitly controlled by the player.

Backward and lateral motion, like acceleration, can also be uncomfortable. In general, try to keep motion along the axis that the player is looking.

Motion is also more comfortable in VR if the player has some control over it. Unexpected motion that are outside the player's control, such as head bobbing, camera shaking, etc, is uncomfortable in VR and should be avoided. Similarly, removing control, such as disabling head tracking will also be uncomfortable. Even if nothing is happening in the game, the player should still be able to look around naturally.

Using 3rd Person for Faster Avatar Motion [edit]

For first person experiences, users tend to prefer slower movement (around a walking pace). If your game need to feature fast turns, acceleration, and jumping, consider switching the perspective to a 3rd person camera that smoothly follows the character. Do not attach the camera to an offset from the character, but rather let the camera float and move at a constant speed to keep up with the character. In this mode it is also important to still let the player freely move their head.

Teleporting [edit]

Another solution to motion is to not provide any interpolated movement at all but instead teleport the player from location to location. Keep in mind this technique has not yet been thoroughly explored, so it is not yet clear if players generally find this solution more comfortable.

Using Vehicles [edit]

Using Vehicles [edit]

Vehicles make a nice setting for a VR experience as the player will often be sitting in real life while playing. Vehicles can also create motion sickness though, so as with character motion you have to be careful with how the vehicle moves. One great rule to follow when adding a vehicle, always make sure some part of the vehicle is visible regardless of where the player looks. This will give the player a static reference they can use to ground themselves.

Performance [edit]

Performance is a critical and foundational element of comfort. If a game jitters or lags, players will likely feel discomfort. It is important to make sure that you develop within the current capabilities of the ROBLOX platform. While developing a VR experience, you will have to be very careful about performance heavy elements, such as player and part count, along with general script overhead.

Presence [edit]

After comfort, presence is the most important consideration in developing a great VR experience. Presence refers to how much the player feels like they are immersed and engaged with their environment. There are several key things that break presence:

- Lack of comfort
- Confusion - what to do, where to go, what's happening
- Shallow object interactions - players expect drawers to open, door knobs to work, etc
- Unintuitive interactions - everyday interactions that work differently in VR than expected
- Too intense - anything that makes someone want to rip off the headset
- Unrealistic audio - not spatially distributed, no distance attenuation
- Proprioceptive disconnect - you are sitting down and your avatar is running

Engagement [edit]

Taken to the extreme, the above ideas suggest that everything in the environment should be fully realized and interactive. While this is a great ambition to strive for, there are many practical considerations that will likely limit your scope (performance, design, engineering hours).

Instead of simply trying to make everything interactive to the extreme, be very deliberate when designing the actions the player can take. If a game is mostly about combat, the player's attention will likely be focused on relevant actions, and not on mundane interactions they might expect the environment to have.

Engagement [edit]

Taken to the extreme, the above ideas suggest that everything in the environment should be fully realized and interactive. While this is a great ambition to strive for, there are many practical considerations that will likely limit your scope (performance, design, engineering hours).

Instead of simply trying to make everything interactive to the extreme, be very deliberate when designing the actions the player can take. If a game is mostly about combat, the player's attention will likely be focused on relevant actions, and not on mundane interactions they might expect the environment to have.

Google's Cardboard Design Lab has some great examples of how you can use visual signals to direct players towards engaging parts of a space. These signals can be subtle (people generally walk towards the light and away from darkness) or more direct (a flashing neon "Open" sign). The proper signaling can lead the player towards engaging activities with interactive 3D objects, and away from visual set pieces that simply create ambiance.

Audio [edit]

Audio cues can be a subtle yet powerful tool to draw players into a VR experience. The key here though is to make use of ROBLOX's positional audio. If an interaction or object makes a sound, the sound should be positioned at the point of interaction. For example, if a player opens a drawer, the Sound instance should be place inside the drawer model.

Try to make ambient noises (such as birds singing, water dripping, generators humming) positioned as well. Even if you don't have specific models for these objects, simply giving them some presence in the environment that changes as the player moves will further the sense of immersion.

GUIs and Text [edit]

2D GUIs drawn directly to the screen should not be used in VR. These both break presence and are uncomfortable. Instead, try to integrate interface elements into the 3D space in your world. The simplest approach is to simply place 2D GUIs on 3D objects like billboards, but there are many creative ways to convey information to your player. Here are some examples:

- Make ammo utilization a gauge on a 3D weapon rather than a 2D HUD
- Replace 2D text boxes with 3D text annotations on objects
- Use a virtual tablet for menu selection rather than a 2D HUD
- Replace a 2D gun target with a 3D laser and reticle projected on the interested object

Intensity [edit]

If a VR experience is very immersive, the intensity of actions and events can be increased. This should be considered when designing a VR experience. A monster jumping at a player

Intensity [edit]

If a VR experience is very immersive, the intensity of actions and events can be increased. This should be considered when designing a VR experience. A monster jumping at a player in VR will be more pronounced in a VR experience if that experience is very immersive. A developer should carefully test and tune their experience and make sure that if the presence in their game is high that they scale back the intensity to preserve player comfort.

Scale [edit]

When building an experience in VR special attention should be given to the scale of buildings and objects. Games in 3rd person typically feature wide spaces and high ceilings to accommodate the camera. In 1st person, these types of spaces can seem unrealistic which can diminish presence. Unless your experience needs to play with scale for narrative or stylistic effects, try to make sure that objects in the experience are scaled to the size of the player's character.

The default ROBLOX character model does not follow standard human proportions, so figuring out scale can be tricky at first glance. It is recommended to start with the vertical size of objects with the height of the character. Then, adjust the horizontal size to balance realism while still accommodating the width of the character. For default sized ROBLOX characters, 1 stud should be treated as 30 centimeters.

Sample Places [edit]

The RobloxVR account has many open-sourced VR places you can edit for inspiration and reference. Click here to see all of these sample places.

Further Reading [edit]

- Oculus Published Best Practices
- Cardboard Design Lab App
- Talk by Kimberly Vol about Presence, Comfort, and Intensity
- *I Expect you to Die* VGDC Presentation

Category: VR API

ROBLOX logos, names, and all related indicia are trademarks of ROBLOX Corporation, ©2014.

Privacy Policy   About ROBLOX Wiki   Disclaimers

Next, confirm your selection and enable this setting. You can choose Play on a Roblox game. You'll see a square screen on your monitor indicating VR mode. Now you should be able to put on your headset and play just as you would from any other platform.

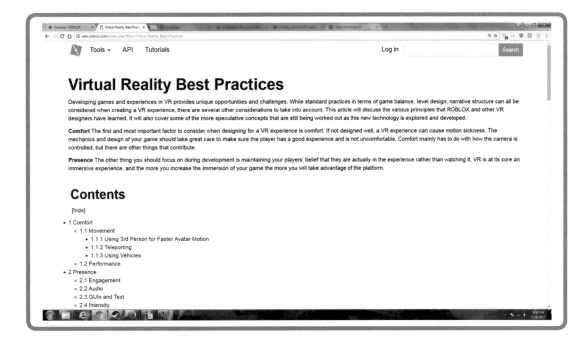

Virtual Reality Best Practices

Developing games and experiences in VR provides unique opportunities and challenges. While standard practices in terms of game balance, level design, narrative structure can all be considered when creating a VR experience, there are several other considerations to take into account. This article will discuss the various principles that ROBLOX and other VR designers have learned. It will also cover some of the more speculative concepts that are still being worked out as this new technology is explored and developed.

Comfort The first and most important factor to consider when designing for a VR experience is comfort. If not designed well, a VR experience can cause motion sickness. The mechanics and design of your game should take great care to make sure the player has a good experience and is not uncomfortable. Comfort mainly has to do with how the camera is controlled, but there are other things that contribute.

Presence The other thing you should focus on during development is maintaining your players' belief that they are actually in the experience rather than watching it. VR is at its core an immersive experience, and the more you increase the immersion of your game the more you will take advantage of the platform.

Contents

[hide]

- 1 Comfort
  - 1.1 Movement
    - 1.1.1 Using 3rd Person for Faster Avatar Motion
    - 1.1.2 Teleporting
    - 1.1.3 Using Vehicles
  - 1.2 Performance
- 2 Presence
  - 2.1 Engagement
  - 2.2 Audio
  - 2.3 GUIs and Text
  - 2.4 Intensity

You can play Roblox games on a number of other devices, including tablets and mobile phones. Playing Roblox from a mobile device is one of the most convenient ways to catch up on your games.

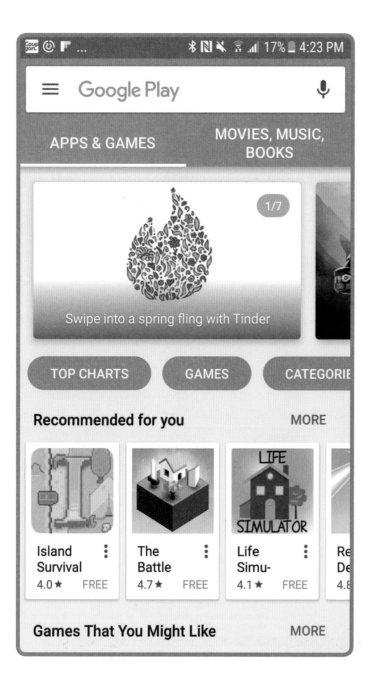

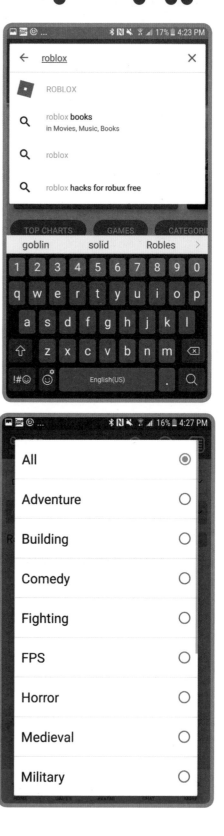

SIGNUP

LOGIN

Username (not your real name)

Password

Confirm password

Gender

Birthday -- -- ----

Cancel

Sign Up

By tapping 'Sign up' above, you are agreeing to our Terms of Service, and Privacy Policy.

Games

Current Balance: R$ 0

Buy ROBUX to customize your avatar and get items in game!

R$ 80	$0.99
R$ 400	$4.99
R$ 800	$9.99
R$ 2,000	$24.99
R$ 4,500	$49.99

HOME   GAMES   AVATAR   CHAT   MORE

ROBLOX

Login

Sign Up

Play Now

Terms of Service - Privacy Policy

Home
hardrockwarrior <13

Customize Your Avatar
Get new clothing in the catalog and customize your avatar.

Build Something
Builders will enjoy playing our multiplayer building game. Professional builders will want to check out ROBLOX Studio, our game development environment on your Develop page

Make Friends

HOME   GAMES   AVATAR   CHAT   MORE

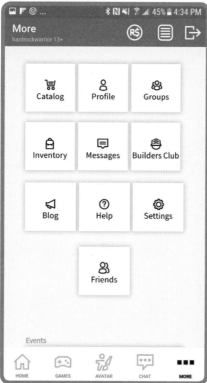

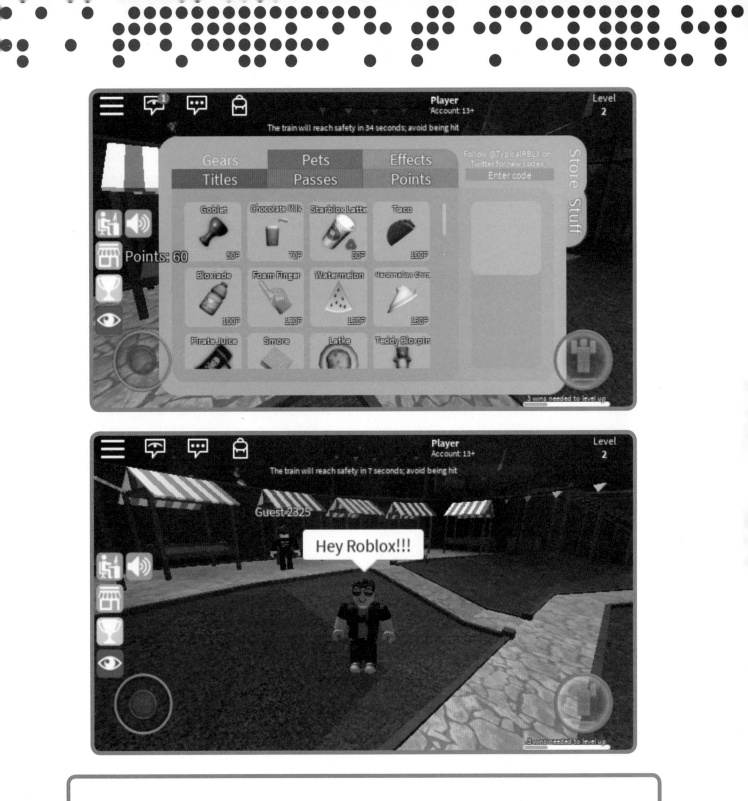

You can currently install Roblox on nearly any mobile device, including those with Apple iOS, Android, and Amazon Fire OS.

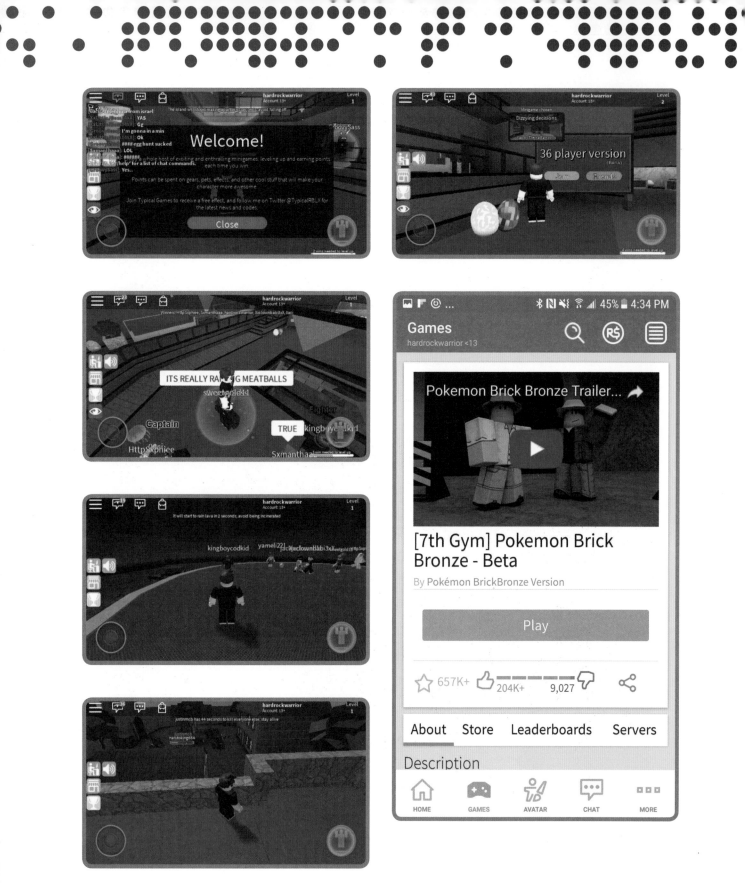

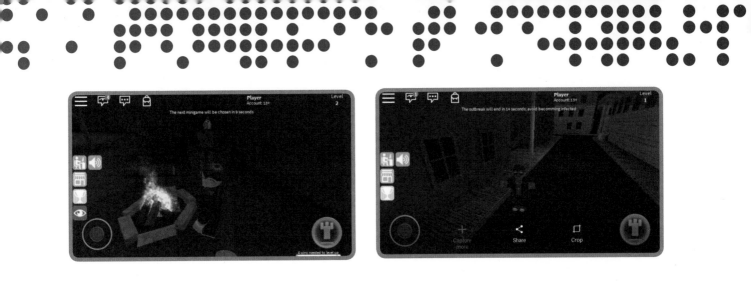

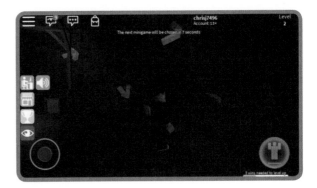

CHAPTER 5

Playing on PC

If you're playing Roblox on a PC, you'll want to install it using your favorite browser. For Google Chrome, you find the game you want to play on the Games page, click on it, and then click the green Play button. You should see a message that says, "You're moments away from getting into the game!" along with a button to download and install Roblox. Once you click the button, downloading will begin.

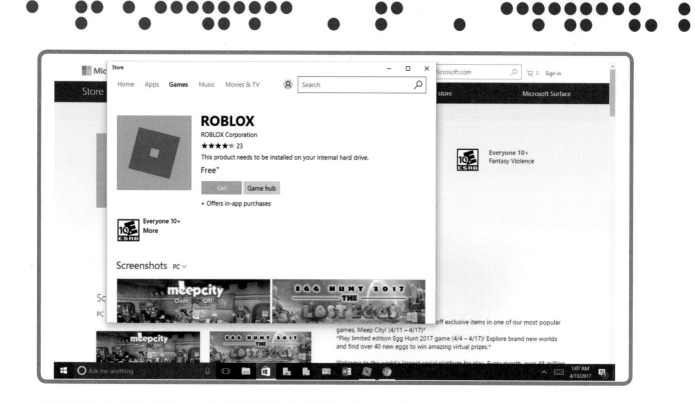

When it's finished downloading, you'll see a screen with instructions for completing the installation. These instructions should say something like:

- In your browser's download bar click RobloxPlayerLauncher.exe to run the Roblox installer.

- When you are prompted, click Run to begin the installation process.

- Click OK once you've successfully installed Roblox.

- Click the green Play button.

Here you'll see the External Protocol Request. Check the box that says, "Remember my choice for all links of this type" and then click Launch Application. Once Roblox is configured, it will open.

The process is similar if you use Microsoft Edge or Mozilla Firefox to install Roblox on a PC.

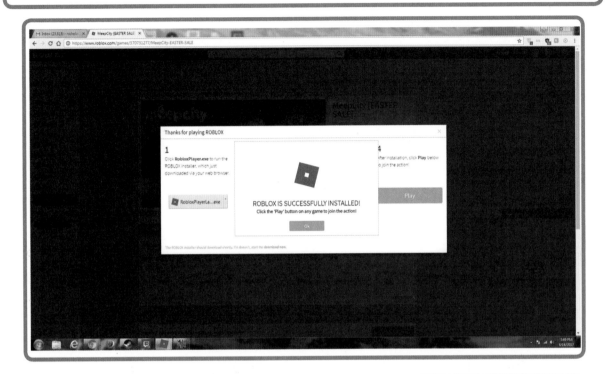

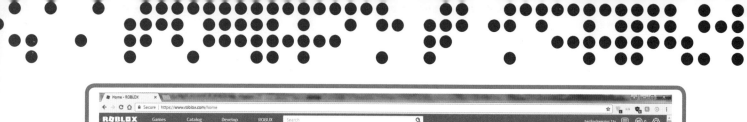

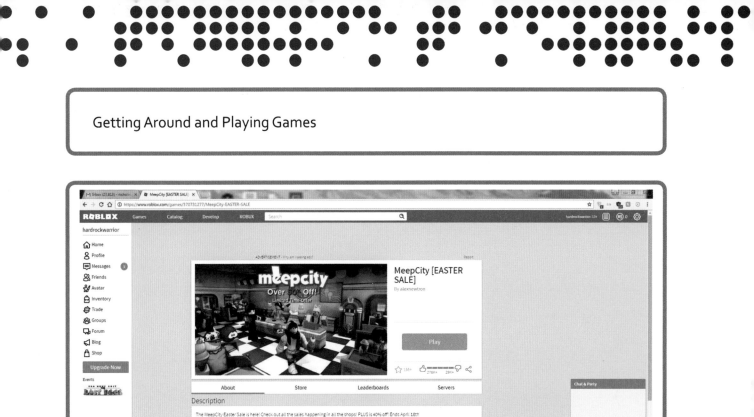

Getting Around and Playing Games

You can move around using the keyboard. W is for Forward, A moves you Left, S is Backward, D moves you Right, and you can use the spacebar to Jump. If you hold the right mouse button down and move the mouse, you can pan the camera. You can also turn the camera left and right. To climb a ladder, simply move toward it using the W key and your character should automatically start climbing it.

Other commands you should get familiar with on the PC are the click, copy, and delete tools. Whenever you come across objects on Roblox, you'll want to use these particular commands. The click tool will move the object and the copy tool will duplicate it. The delete tool will, of course, get rid of the object.

WHEN YOU ARE DONE PLAYING

If you want to leave the game or move to a different world, go to the Menu button at the top left of your screen and press the L key. A window will open to make sure you want to quit the game.

CHATTING ON A PC

You can press the / key to chat. This will open a window where you can chat with other people on the server. Keep in mind that developers of the world can disable this feature if they don't want to enable chat. You can also chat by clicking on the chat screen that says "Click here" if chat is enabled.

CHAPTER 6

Setting Up Your Profile and Avatar

[Unusuals] Ripull Games
By Ripull

Now that you have Roblox installed on your preferred device, you can get started building fun and awesome games. But wait! One of the first things many gamers want to do is choose an avatar and start setting up their personal space on their profile.

When you have your account set up, you can begin to work on creating an interesting profile. Keep in mind that the profile you set up is basically all about you. This is what people will see when they message you and view the things you've created, so you want to make sure it's something you're proud of and that it shows off your personality.

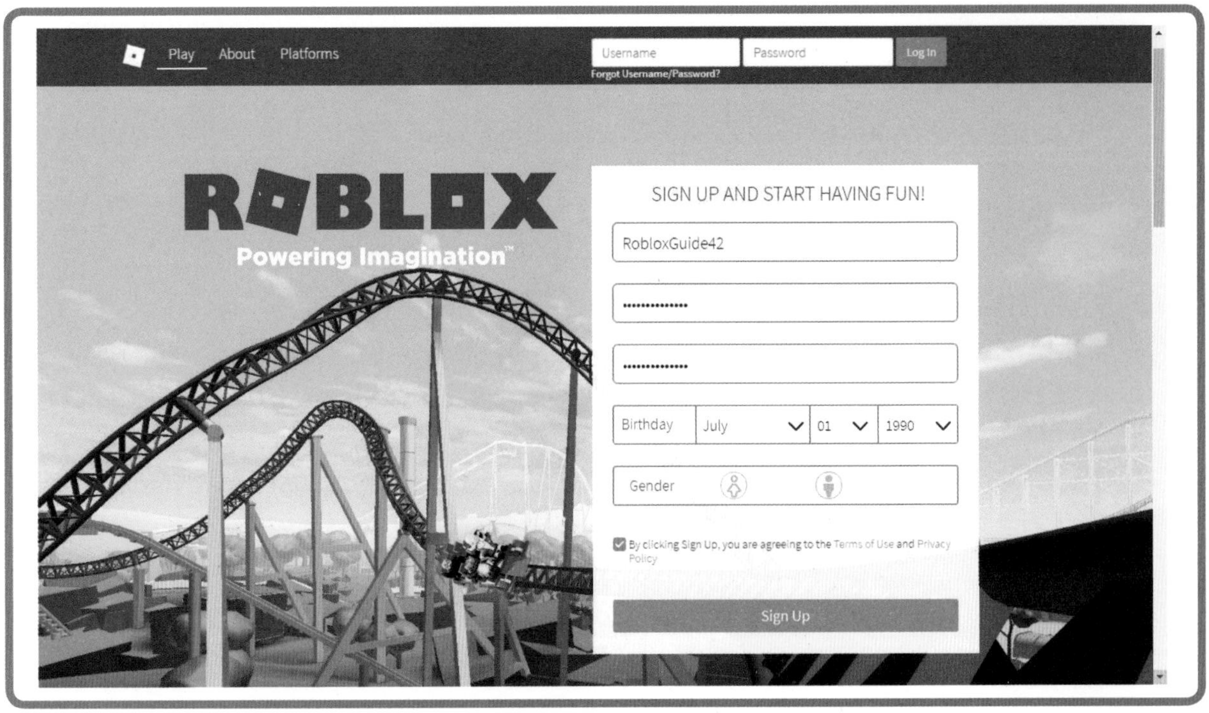

VIEWING YOUR PROFILE

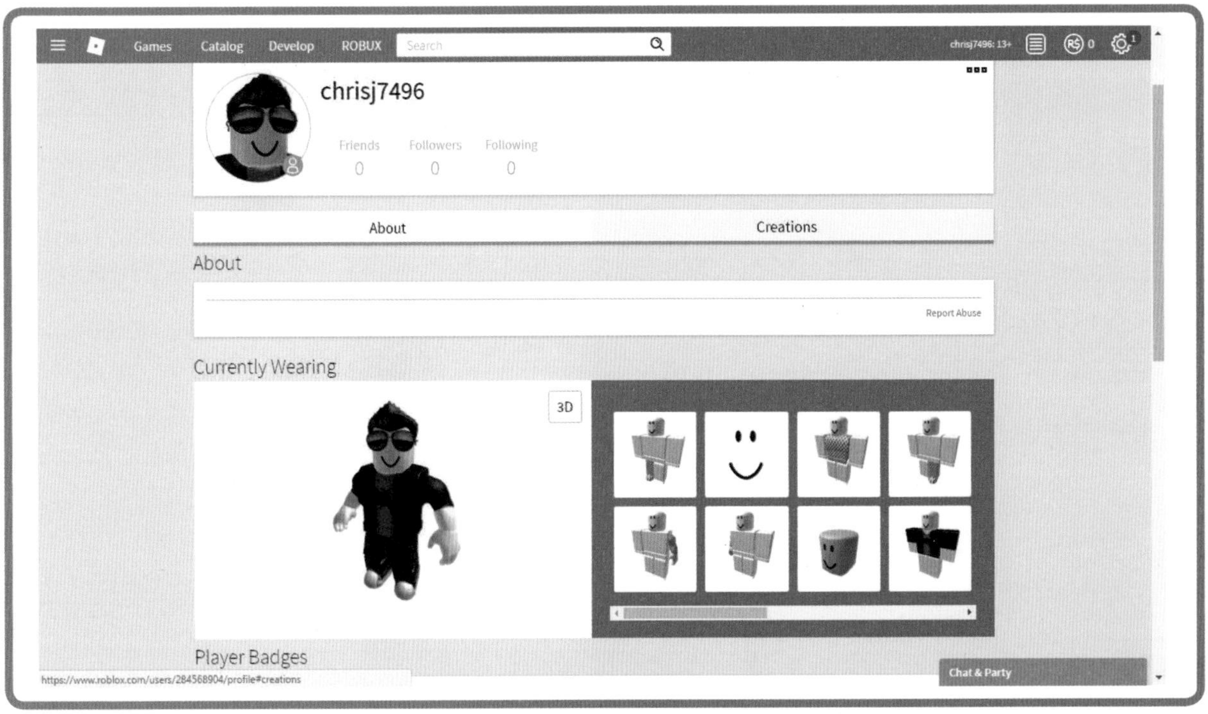

If you want to take a look at your own profile, you simply click the profile icon on the navigation menu on the left side of the page. To view other people's profiles, you can either use the search box if you have the name of the profile or select Search in People. You should see their name pop up in the user list, and then you can click on it to view the profile.

If you want to view the profile of a game or its creator, you can go to the game's Details page and click on their name, located beneath the title. For items, the Details page and name are located at the right.

Once you've found the profile you want to view, you will see a basic information box that tells you the user's name, BC level, and most recent status update. You will also see the user's player icon, friend and follower information, and interaction options.

Are you interested in seeing what they've created? You can click on the Creations tab below the basic information box; this shows you all the interesting things that user has created within the category.

MANAGING YOUR OWN CREATIONS TAB

You might find after you get started on Roblox that you prefer showing off certain creations more than others. In order to manage your own Creations tab and control what others see about you, showcase the creations you are most proud of by going to the game or item's Details page. Then you need to select the gear icon to the right of the title, and from the pop-up menu you can select either Add to Profile or Remove from Profile.

FILLING OUT YOUR ABOUT TAB

You might want to give other players a little extra information about yourself. Do you have a funny quote you'd like to share? Or do you want to create a short and witty blurb about yourself? You can add your blurb or change the one you already have on the About tab of your profile. To do this, you simply need to log in to your account, select the gear icon at the top right of the page, and choose Settings from the pop-up menu. You should see your Personal Blurb box, where you can type something interesting about yourself.

Next to your blurb, you will see an area where you can also add and link any social networks that you might be a part of online. However, you have to be 13 years of age or older to add social networks to your profile on the Social tab. As a reminder, your blurb also must meet Roblox privacy rules and not contain any personally identifiable details about you.

CURRENTLY WEARING SECTION

In the Currently Wearing section of your profile, you will see how your avatar currently looks. You can view either 2D or 3D by clicking on the button at the top of the image. You can also see everything a user is wearing in the blue box to the right. Do you like something another player is wearing? You can click on it here to either buy one for yourself or get more details.

GETTING AROUND THE OTHER SECTIONS OF THE ABOUT TAB

There's much more in your About tab that you might want to take a second to navigate through. For example, you can check out Friends lists, where up to nine of a player's friends will be displayed. If you have more than nine friends, you can see them all by clicking the See All button.

There are other interesting sections you should check out while you're in the About Me section. You'll find more details on these features in later chapters.

COLLECTIONS

Here you can see up to six items that a player most recently obtained. The player can choose the items they want to display if they prefer to show items that were purchased earlier. If you want to view someone's entire inventory by category, you can click on the Inventory button.

If you want to choose what people see in your Collections bar, you can go to your own Details page, select the gear icon on the right, and in the pop-up menu select Add to Profile or Remove from Profile. This gives you some control over the specific items that are displayed in your profile.

GROUPS

In this section, you can view all the groups that a player is part of. This section is similar to the Games section you see in the Creations tab, in that you can see the groups in a detailed view, focusing on one at a time. When you use the arrow icons on the sides of description box, you can scroll through them. There is also an icon you can click if you prefer to see more than one group at once.

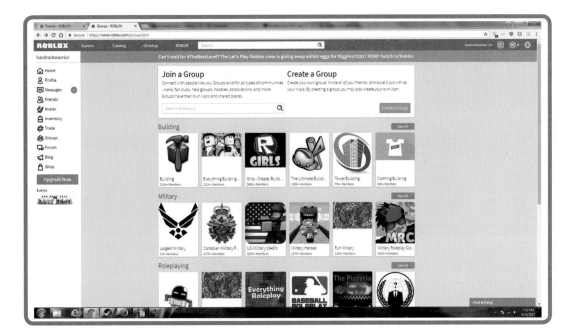

STATISTICS

Here you can view statistics about a player, like when they joined Roblox, how many posts they've made in the forum, the number of people who have visited their places, and many others.

FAVORITE GAMES

This section is where you see all the games a player has favorited. You just need to click the blue Favorites button. While you're playing, you can select a game to favorite yourself for your own section by first going to the Details page of the place you want to favorite. There you can click the star underneath the Play button, which will change from being just outlined to filled in. If you decide you want to unfavorite the game, you just click the button again to return to an outlined star.

Favoriting a game can make it easier to find above your feed. You can also find your favorites on your Home page, under Recently Played, if you select the My Favorite filter on the Games page.

BADGES

You can earn Roblox Badges and Player Badges. In this section, you can see a list of all the Roblox-created badges, as well as how they were obtained. You can also view Player Badges that have been obtained through different actions in particular games. If you want to see how to earn a badge, you can click on it.

CHOOSING YOUR AVATAR

Next up, personalizing your Roblox avatar. Depending on whether you want your character to look like you or someone completely different, you have lots of options when you choose your avatar.

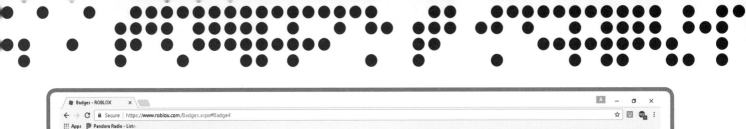

To get started with choosing your avatar, you need to click on Avatar in the navigation menu on the left side of the page. If for some reason you don't see the menu, you might need to click the menu icon (three stacked lines) in the top left corner to make it visible.

SELECTING YOUR AVATAR'S GENDER

When you first set up your Roblox avatar, you can choose its gender right away. However, you might find that you either accidentally chose the wrong one or you wish to change it later. All you need to do to change the gender that was selected is edit it on your Account Settings page. Click on the gear icon in the top right corner and select Settings, and then make your change. This will change the gender on the Roblox account registration, but it won't change the appearance of your avatar.

To modify how your avatar looks, you can choose one of the free packages from the catalog. Currently, there is a Roblox Man Package, a Roblox Woman Package, and a Roblox Girl Package. Once you've selected the package you want, you can just go to the Avatar page, click Packages from the categories on the right, and then select Wear to update your character's look.

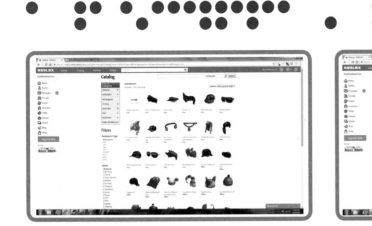

WHAT WILL YOUR AVATAR WEAR?

You can then view the available options for making changes to your avatar. For example, under the Wardrobe tab, you can change clothes or items such as the avatar's head, arms and gear. If you have multiple items, such as hats, you can go through the pages until you find the item you want. Once you choose the item you want to add to the avatar, click the Wear button next to it.

The Outfits feature in Roblox allows you to create customized outfits and save them to change into later by storing multiple configurations. First you need to go to the Avatar section, then you can add or remove items until you like how the avatar looks, and then click the Outfits tab. Once you've clicked Create New Outfit, you can enter a name for it (as a label of sorts) and click Create. After you have created a new Outfit, you can select options like Wear, Rename, Update, and Delete by clicking on the gear icon on the right. This way, you'll always have a catalog of options to choose from, depending on your mood – with the ability to create and store up to 50 custom outfits on your account!

You'll likely find yourself adding and removing items until you find the perfect look. To remove something, you can go to Currently Wearing and cycle through the pages until you find the item you want to remove from your avatar, then simply click the Remove button. Sometimes your avatar might not display the item correctly. If this happens, you can select the button that says, "Click here to re-draw it!" to refresh the image.

CHANGING YOUR AVATAR'S SKIN COLOR

Besides choosing clothing and other items for your avatar, you can also select how you want your character to appear, right down to its skin color. Go to the Avatar section on the left side after you have logged in to your account. Scroll down until you see an outline of a Roblox avatar under your avatar. You can click on the body part whose skin color you want to change, and then a box will appear with a

list of colors to choose from. You will need to repeat this process for each part of the body that you want to change.

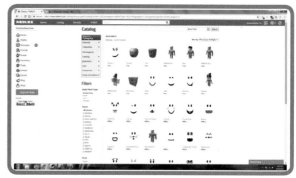

It is recommended that if you change to outfits with unique body colors, you always save them so you can get them back in the future. Otherwise, when there are changes or updates made to the Avatar Editor, you risk losing features like this.

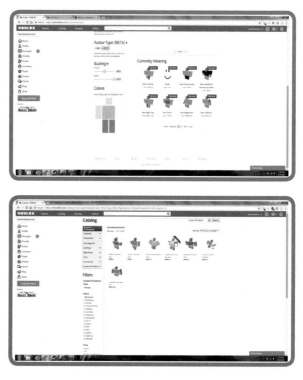

HOW DO I GET BADGES?

As mentioned earlier, there are two kinds of badges you can add to your Roblox account: Roblox Badges and Player Badges. Many players see these badges as a representation of your accomplishments. You can earn badges by completing different tasks or by interacting with Roblox in different ways. You can view the badges earned in the Badges section of Inventory, and if you want to see how a particular badge was earned, you can click on it to read its description.

Here are some of the Roblox Badges you can earn, and how to earn them.

MEMBERSHIP BADGES

The membership badges are awarded to players who become members of the various Roblox clubs that are available to join.

- **Welcome to the Club Badge:** You can earn this badge if you belong to Builders Club. We'll cover everything you need to know about Builders Club in Chapter 15.

- **Builders Club Badge:** This badge is also awarded when you become a member of Builders Club.

- **Turbo Builders Club Badge:** Members of the Turbo Builders Club are considered some of the most dedicated Roblox members. You earn this badge when you become a member. This club is also covered in more detail in Chapter 15.

- **Outrageous Builders Club Badge:** Outrageous Builders Club members are considered Roblox VIPs, or "the cream of the crop." This badge basically indicates that someone is one of the top-level Roblox members, and this membership is covered in Chapter 15 as well.

COMMUNITY BADGES

These are badges you can earn as part of the community. They also help identify certain people in the community and those who have been part of certain programs in the past.

- **Administrator Badge:** If you see this badge, it means that the person is a Roblox administrator. Only official administrators have this badge, so if you meet someone who claims to be an admin but doesn't have this badge, you should report the account as abuse and Roblox will delete the imposter's account.

- **Veteran Badge:** Members who have played Roblox for one year or longer earn the Veteran Badge. Roblox considers these players to be loyal members who have stuck with the community and helped make it the game it is today. According to Roblox, "These medalists are the true steel, the core of Robloxian history...and its future."

- **Friendship Badge:** Players who have embraced the Roblox community and made at least 20 friends earn the Friendship Badge. This can help you identify people who may be able to help you out if you're having trouble.

- **Ambassador Badge:** You probably won't see this badge often, because it was awarded to players during the Ambassador Program, which only ran from 2009 to 2012. This badge has been retired and is no longer attainable.

- **Inviter Badge:** Another badge you won't see often is the Inviter Badge, which was awarded during the Inviter Program from 2009 to 2013. This badge has also been retired and is no longer attainable.

DEVELOPER BADGES

One of the fun features of Roblox is the ability to develop and create your own worlds. The developer badges are awarded to players who create popular places and communities on Roblox.

- **Homestead Badge:** When your personal place has been visited at least 100 times, you earn the Homestead Badge. If you see a player with this badge, it means they've been able to show that they can build impressive things on Roblox that other people were interested in and took the time to check out. To earn this badge faster, you can invite people to visit your place.

- **Bricksmith Badge:** If you have a popular personal place that has been visited at least 1,000 times, you can earn this badge. This award is typically earned by players who have created places that people have checked out thousands of times, and who are considered experts when it comes to putting bricks together.

- **Official Model Maker Badge:** This badge is considered one of the most prestigious, because it's awarded to players who have made such amazing creations that Roblox has endorsed them. This badge usually indicates that the player has elevated talent in scripting and building.

GAMER BADGES

These badges were awarded to players in certain games.

- **Combat Initiation Badge:** If you scored 10 victories in games using classic combat scripts, you would have earned this badge. However, it is no longer available, having been retired during the summer of 2015.

- **Warrior Badge:** This badge was also retired in the summer of 2015. It indicated that a player had scored 100 or more victories in games using classic combat scripts.

- **Bloxxer Badge:** Also retired and no longer available, the Bloxxer Badge was awarded when a player scored at least 250 victories with fewer than 250 wipeouts in classic combat scripted games.

Although some of the badges that you might see are no longer awarded to players, they give you an indication of a player's strengths and accomplishments in the past. New Roblox programs and achievement opportunities are always being launched, so you should keep your eye out for new ways to earn badges.

Did you know you can make a shirt in Roblox? You'll be surprised at how easy it is, actually. Once you have Builders Club, you can work in the Roblox textile mill and make pants and shirts for yourself and to sell to other players. Depending on your fashion sense and artistic skills, you could end up racking up Robux to pay for other things.

Although you can always buy shirts and pants from the catalog, many players enjoy being able to create and sell their own Roblox clothing. Here's how to get started making your own new clothes.

You can use a variety of image editing programs to create your shirt design, depending on what you're most comfortable working with. There are plenty of programs, like Microsoft Paint and Gimp, that you can use for free.

When you've finished your shirt design, go to the Develop page, which you can select from the right side of the Roblox logo at the top left. Select either Shirts or Pants, depending on your preference, from the tabs on the left side. If you're making a shirt, for example, you need to download the shirt template, which is a picture you draw on to create your shirt.

Click Build New and Create a Shirt. Under Create a Shirt you should see, "Did you use the template? If not, download it." This is where you download the template so you can design your clothing. When you click on the link, the template will open in a new tab and you can right-click on it to save it to your computer.

It might take a second to get used to working with the Shirt Template on Roblox. You'll see a bunch of shapes and colors, which can become a bit overwhelming to even the most seasoned gamers. The good news is you'll get the hang of using the template in no time, and soon you'll be able to say you have experience as a 3D graphic artist.

One helpful note to keep in mind when you design your shirt is that the arms are labeled opposite to the actual. What is referred to as the right arm in the template is actually the left, which you'll want to remember if your design includes anything you want specifically on the right or left arm.

Luckily, you can use one template for both the shirt and the pants, so once you get accustomed to it, you'll find creating clothing for your character a breeze. It's important to note that the image you upload has to have the same dimensions as the template, which are approximately 585 pixels by 559 pixels, or the upload will fail.

If you decide that it's easier to work on each part by itself, the dimensions are as follows:

- Squares are 128x128 pixels, used for the front and back of the torso.
- Skyscraper rectangles are 64x128 pixels, used for torso sides and arm and leg sides.
- Banner rectangles are 64x128 pixels, used for the top and bottom of the torso.
- Small squares are 64x64 pixels, used for the top and bottom of arms and legs.

UNDERSTANDING THE LIMITATIONS OF TEMPLATES

You'll need to be aware of the limitations of the templates when you create your clothing. For example, because the arms and legs bend, you have to make sure you check how much space things like the shoes will take up. If the shoes are too high on your pants template, you could see parts of them when the leg bends at the top. This is something to check when it comes to all bendable areas of pants as well as shirts.

Once you've painted your shirt, you can upload it. Select Choose File to select your shirt and click Upload. The shirt will then show up in your wardrobe.

SELLING YOUR SHIRTS ON ROBLOX

You can wear your clothing, or you can sell your shirts on Roblox to other players. If you want, you can advertise your newly created shirt by clicking the title of the shirt from Create a Shirt or Inventory or Character. When you see the page with the title of your shirt at the top, you can select Configure and then Advertise. You have a variety of ad options, including a Banner, a Skyscraper, and a Rectangle. You can create your ad, customize it, and then click Choose File and Upload. Here you can also bid a price with tickets or Robux for the ad, which will run for 24 hours before it is taken down.

CHAPTER 8

Earning, Spending, and Using Robux

By this point, you've read about Robux more than once. You're probably wondering how on earth you can earn Robux and what exactly you would do with them anyway. In short, Robux is the virtual currency that is used in Roblox and many of its online games. It started as Roblox Points in the beginning of 2006 and was later replaced with Robux. Robux are awarded to users and developers, and can be used to purchase items for your avatar and cool gear to help you out in multiplayer battles. You can also convert Robux to cash through the Developer Exchange program.

HOW TO GET ROBUX

Starter Kit provides 400 Robux for $4.95, up to 2,000 Robux for $24.95. There is also a Super Value option that starts at 4,500 Robux for $49.95 and goes up to as many as 22,500 for $199.95. Each level also offers a special bonus if you decide to sign up for Builders Club. (Of course, make sure you ask your parents or guardian and have permission before you make any Robux purchases.)

There are a bunch of ways to earn Robux. One of the easiest ways is to become a Builders Club member, which includes a daily Robux stipend, depending on your membership. You don't have to do anything else – you just automatically earn Robux every day with your membership. As a member, you can also sell items such as shirts, pants, and place access to earn a 70 percent profit on the Robux, which can quickly add up. Plus, when you first sign up for Builders Club, there is a signing bonus of 100 Robux.

Another way to get Robux is by purchasing from the Robux page. Sometimes there are special offers and deals that you can get when you purchase your Robux here. Right now, the

creation page to get started. You can get to this page by going to your profile page and selecting Create a Game Pass under your active places, or you can go to the Develop page and select the configuration from the dropdown menu.

SELLING GAME PASSES FOR ROBUX

Whether you are a Builders Club member or not, you can sell Game Passes to earn Robux. Game Passes are like VIP shirts that give players special perks and abilities in Roblox games, such as super strength or speed, or even a special item, depending on the game creator's preference. You can create Game Passes for free, but you can sell them for whatever amount you choose. The Robux you earn from Game Passes are held for up to three business days and are subject to a transaction fee. If you are not a Builders Club member, you get 10 percent of the profit while members earn 70 percent of the profit.

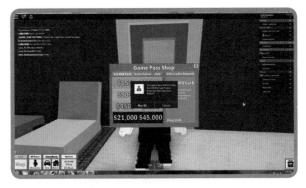

CREATING A GAME PASS

If you want to create a Game Pass to earn Robux, you will need to go to the Game Pass

You can then follow the directions for creating your Game Pass. Basically, this means you need to first download the Badge Template, then fill the white area with your badge, and then fill out the form for your image, including a place name and an interesting name. Make sure you also add a description of the Game Pass, and then select Verify.

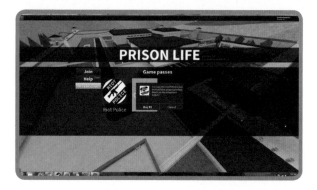

RAKE IN THE ROBUX AND SELL YOUR GAME PASS

Once you've created your Game Pass, you can get started selling it and earning Robux. It won't show up on your place right away because it will need to be on sale or available for free. Go to the Game Pass page and select Configure This Game Pass from the Options button at the top right. Once you select the configure option, you can sell the Game Pass. Make sure you save your changes when you're done. Don't forget you can also purchase Game Passes from other players by simply navigating to their places' pages and selecting Buy Now when you see the icon, name, and description of the pass you want.

SHARE YOUR FAVORITE PAGE AND EARN ROBUX

Both members and nonmembers can also earn Robux by participating in the Affiliate Program. This basically means you can earn Robux by spreading the word and sharing Roblox with your friends and family members. The Roblox Affiliate Program allows you to generate a link to a Roblox page that you can share. This page can be a game, a hat, or anything on the site that you think your friends might be interested in. If another player visits the site through your link and then creates an account, you will earn a 5 percent bonus on any Robux they buy in the future. For example, if your best friend sees your link, clicks on it, opens a Roblox account, and then buys 2,000 Robux to get started, you would get a 5 percent bonus of 2,000 Robux – that's 100 Robux just for sharing the game! What's even better is that you earn this 5 percent bonus every time your friend makes a purchase.

CREATING YOUR AFFILIATE LINK

You can create your link by clicking on the social media button on any page you want to share from the site and selecting the network you want to post it on. You can share your affiliate link on Facebook, Twitter, your website, or anywhere else that someone interested in Roblox might see it. If you don't see a social media button on the page, you can go to the Trade section of the navigation bar on the left side, click on the Promotions tab, paste the URL into the Roblox URL box,

and when the link is automatically generated, copy and share it. You can view the Robux you've earned from your affiliate links on your Trade section's summary tab, on the line that says, "Promoted Page Conversion Revenue."

EARN ROBUX WITH DEVELOPER ATTRIBUTION

One other way to earn Robux is called Developer Attribution. This feature can be particularly beneficial for developers who build games that are successful at converting visitors to purchases. Through Developer Attribution, Roblox tracks visitors who go from your page to register for an account, as well as those registered users who also make purchases of Robux or Builders Club memberships. When people make purchases, the developer earns 5 percent of the purchase.

This process is similar to the Affiliate Program but instead helps game developers earn income by creating successful games. It also inspires developers to share and promote their games through social media, advertising, and PR. So, even if you do not monetize your games or share affiliate links from Roblox pages, you can earn Robux from the people who play your games.

You can view your stats under Developer Stats for each game. A chart titled, "Game Page Conversion Revenue" will show you how many people have registered after landing on your page, as well as the money you have earned from those visitors.

WHAT TO WATCH OUT FOR WHEN LOOKING FOR ROBUX

There have been accounts of scams where a person, website, or game claims to be a Robux Generator or able to get you free Robux. Such claims are not true, and you should report them to Roblox through its Report Abuse system if you encounter anything like this.

CHAPTER 9

Building Awesome Games

Part of the fun of Roblox is not just setting up your place and your character and playing games, but also being able to build your own awesome games. Using the Roblox Studio and the programming language Lua to change the environment of the game, there's really nothing you can't create with Roblox.

CREATING PLACES

You can compare Roblox places to levels, and games are made up of these places or levels. When you are creating places, you will select File, then New in the Studio, or you will select a template. After you edit a place, you can publish it as part of a new game or you can add it to an existing game.

You will also need to create a Start Place, which every game on Roblox must have to give players a place to begin when they first enter the game. Then players can move to other places in the game using the Teleport Service. To make things a bit easier when you create games in Roblox, though, if a place is published to a new game, it will automatically become the Start Place. Once others are added to the game, you can use Game Explorer to change the Start Place in Studio, or through the game's configuration on the website.

You can use the Roblox Studio building system to create places with bricks of many colors and shapes – just as if you were building and creating in real life. You can also choose from a variety of plugins and tools to build whatever you can imagine. If you want, you can scroll through the Roblox Library to look for models and scripts – many of which are free.

Plus, Roblox's Official Model Maker system is available if you want to create places and make your creations appear on the front page of the Roblox Library model section. You can get access to plugins developed with Lua that you can use in the Studio as well.

HOW TO START BUILDING A GAME

First you will need to launch the Roblox Studio and select the Baseplate option. If you click Model on the top bar, you can choose the bricks you want to build with. The basic blocks you will be using the most for inserting are referred to as Parts.

You can also use free models, which are available when you make the Toolbox sidebar visible in the Window menu. However, it's recommended that you try to make your own models and avoid free models that might have infected scripts. These scripts can spread outside the model and affect the rest of your game.

Even if you don't use any of the free models, it's helpful to make your Toolbox sidebar visible. You can begin adding bricks, models, and anything else you want in your game. It's helpful to group blocks together to keep everything organized. To do this, select each block you want to group, right click, and select Group from the menu. When you're finished building and grouping, you can select Publish to Roblox. Because it's possible to spend quite a bit of time making your creations, don't risk losing all your hard work.

It's important to make sure you save a backup copy throughout your work session. You can save by going to File, Save As, and entering the name of your place. When you press Enter, your game will be saved. Saving throughout can help prevent you from accidentally publishing after you've inserted an infected free model. Instead, you can load an earlier saved version that has not been infected, saving yourself a great deal of disappointment and frustration.

INSERTING PLUGINS: FOR ADVANCED PLAYERS

If you are somewhat more advanced in building games in Roblox, you can use this method to build and insert plugins as well. Plugins are packs of tools designed to help players create more than just a basic project. You can search for plugins to use as building tools in the Roblox Library, and here are some others you might want to try:

- Building Tools by F3X, which allows more advanced builders to include details that can't be created with basic tools.

- GapFill fills in different gaps, especially those that are in atypical or complex shapes.

- Oozledraw Toolbar – Draw Curve/Rope allows you to make curves using geometry according to the gravity pull, the kind, and the form for making rope or adding more detail to something.

- Cutscene Editor for making tours of your places by showing how players can go from one point to another and where you are facing.

Once you have found a plugin you like, you can click the Favorite button or Take One. You will then need to launch Roblox Studio and start a completely fresh copy. This won't work if you attempt to use a window you've already opened a build in. When Roblox Studio begins, you will see a Web browser inside the studio with an address bar at the top. In this browser, near the tabs where you would normally switch between script and place editing, you should type www.roblox.com and log in (if you are not using Internet Explorer).

While you're inside this browser, you can go to your profile and scroll to the bottom, where a new Plugins category will appear because of the plugin you favorited. Here it's also a good idea to save if you have any builds open in the Studio. Select the favorited plugin, which should cause the Install button to turn from dark to green. When you click it, Roblox Studio will restart and install your plugin. When the installation is finished, right-click the toolbars at the top, where you should see a new unchecked toolbar. Click to turn it on and then either open a place or create a new one, according to the options you are provided.

CREATING A GREAT PLACE ON ROBLOX

It's possible to create a great place that impresses other players and gets you lots of visitors. Creating a place that gets you famous includes some of the following steps. First, go to the place you want to edit and select Develop and Edit to get started. Open Roblox Studio and insert a part. After clicking it once, you will need to go to the top left of your screen to View and then Properties. Here you should find Anchored, and then make it True and the top and bottom surfaces Smooth.

Next, click the part again, and at the top left of your screen, go to Insert and Object. You can then find Blockmesh and insert it into the selected brick. This gives you the option to resize your part, recolor it, or build anything else you choose. Don't forget to use properties such as transparency and reflection to get it to look exactly how you want.

You can create new bricks by clicking Insert at the top left corner, then selecting Bricks from the menu and clicking the color you want. You can move bricks with the Game Tool and by clicking and holding the mouse button on the brick. Rotate your brick by pressing R; tilt it by pressing T.

To edit your bricks, go to Roblox Studio and click on Edit Mode in the toolbar. When Explorer opens on the right side of your screen, you will see a list of every object you've found in the game. Edit your blocks by opening Workspace, pressing the + button, and editing the properties of the bricks. You can edit the shape, color, and size of the blocks by pressing Resize.

Save your place by clicking Edit Mode, File, and Publish to Roblox. This will also share your place with the public and store it on the Roblox server so other players can visit it. If you want to save it to your computer so you can edit it later, click File and then Save As and type the name of your place.

OTHER NOTES TO KEEP IN MIND FOR SUCCESSFUL BUILDING

If you're making a combat game, you should make a round-system. If it's a tycoon, you need to make sure you have enough tycoons. With an obby, you want to stick to blue, green, and brown tints and avoid using too many colors. This is because reds can anger players when they don't win, while blues and greens might keep them calm.

It's also important to make sure, if it's a minigame, that it actually works and doesn't make you wait too long. For the most popular games, you should make sure disaster games are difficult enough and don't make the player wait an eternity for every disaster. If it's another type of game, make sure there is something to do. One of the downfalls of many Roblox hangouts is that there aren't enough activities.

It's also recommended that you add badges for the most difficult tasks to encourage players to play the game. You can also attract players with badges for things such as Welcome, Winner (if your level is an obby), VIP, and Mega VIP. Keep in mind that you need to be a member of Builders Club to make and upload badges to your places.

Above all, make sure your game doesn't break or lag, which can frustrate gamers. In order to attract visitors and players, you might want to play with your friends. This also gives you a chance to make sure everything is working properly. You can also attract more players by sharing your game and advertising. No matter what you create in Roblox, remember to have fun and let your imagination run wild.

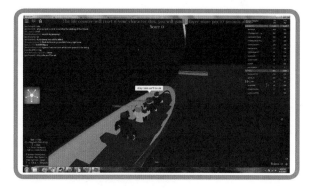

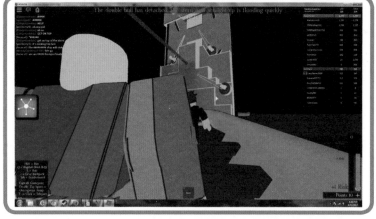

CHAPTER 10
Multiple Places

There was a time when Roblox was only one place, with copies of that one place created whenever it filled with players. However, too many parts slowed down places and limited the details of the environment. This is referred to as a game or as a universe. However, now games can consist of multiple places so that players can move easily between places within a game. It also means larger and more detailed worlds, involving towns surrounded by caves and forests, and the ability to transport between each place.

MANAGING MULTIPLE PLACES

You can go to the Roblox website to change the Start Place and add other places to a game. First you need to log in to Roblox and then click Develop. Select Games from the list, which opens a list of all your places. The current Start Place will be under each game on the list. Click Configure to edit the game information. You can change the name of the game on the Basic Settings tab, and change the Start Place at the Places tab. The Created Places tab will list the specific instances created in this game.

CHAPTER 11
Body Movers

Body Movers are a new feature in the Roblox Studio. These movers include advanced user capabilities and functionality. You can still do everything you could before with movers, but the new movers offer improved performance. To create Body Movers in the Studio, you will first need to go to the Create menu in the Constraint group on the Model tab.

You will need two clicks on two parts of AlignOrientation, AlignPosition, and LineForce, which will create the mover with two attachments. The first click is for attachment0 and the second is for attachment1. The mover object will be parented to the first part clicked.

Next, VectorForce and Torque need only one click to create the mover and a single attachment. You can also preselect attachments before you choose your mover. This creates the Mover/Constraint with the preselected attachments. You can see the visual representations of the Movers when you press the Show Details button. Movers can be selected when you click on their visual representations, and when a move is selected, the associated attachments are highlighted to show relevant information.

There are many different game categories that you should become familiar with, including tycoons, shooters, RPGs (Role Playing Games), and many others. Some of the most popular game genres are the following:

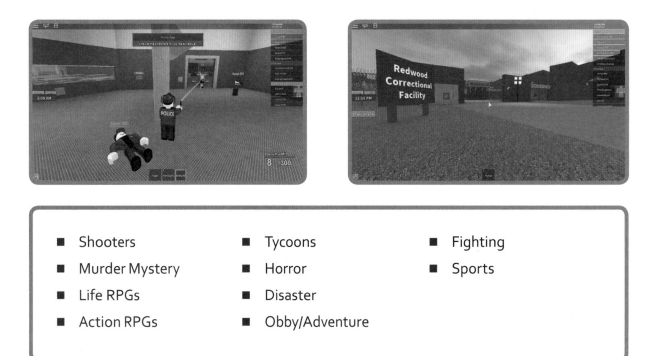

- Shooters
- Murder Mystery
- Life RPGs
- Action RPGs

- Tycoons
- Horror
- Disaster
- Obby/Adventure

- Fighting
- Sports

Here's a more in-depth explanation of some of the game categories that can help you get a better idea of what's available in Roblox.

WHAT ARE TYCOONS?

One of the most popular Roblox games ever created, Bread Factory Tycoon, ended up getting more than 500,000 visits in 2007. The scripter, referred to as Uber, decided to uncopylock the game so other players could use it. This led to scripters creating their own tycoons and even a tycoon kit, which helps players create tycoons.

HOW TO START A TYCOON

To start a tycoon, you will most likely need to walk around until you find a vacant building, which is typically a door or button. You can claim a tycoon by walking or bumping into the button or door, depending on the layout.

In most tycoons, you will find an automatic machine called a dropper, which is used for producing bricks. There are three parts of a machine: the brick producer, the conveyor belt, and the brick collector, each of which has its own purpose. The brick producer places the bricks on the conveyor belt, which transports the bricks. The brick collector removes the bricks and gives money in exchange. You might also run into a button called an upgrader, a button that can make another machine, a button that can make the bricks move faster, or a button that will give you more money for each brick.

MINING TYCOONS OR LUMBER TYCOONS

In mining or lumber tycoons the player has to work manually. You will usually have a tool that you will need to approach an object with and then you ram or stab the object with the tool.

AUTO CASH

Some tycoons have cash that's automatically delivered to the player. The more things you buy, the faster the cash goes.

HOW TO GET AN UPGRADE

Upgrades can be for money-making, for recreation, or for decoration. To get an upgrade, you usually have to step on a button that removes the money from the player, puts the upgrade into the game, and removes the button. In games like Lumber Tycoon II, you buy upgrades in the form of boxes and take them to the player's lot.

DONATING TO TYCOONS

In order to donate, you almost always have to use a button on the screen. In some games, you can donate using a tool, which can help players who need loans.

COMPLETING THE GAME

When a player purchases the last upgrade, the game ends. Usually, this last upgrade is something expensive, like a statue. However, like most games on Roblox, the game keeps going until the player leaves. Sometimes you might get a badge when you complete the tycoon.

If you find that tycoons are your preferred type of game, make sure you check out Roblox events such as the recent Innovation Tycoon Event. In this event, the most popular tycoon games were updated, and players were offered opportunities to take on challenges and win free virtual items and prizes. The popular tycoon games that were part of this event included Theme Park Tycoon, which offered a chance to win an exclusive accessory for your avatar; Retail Tycoon, which offered a special virtual item for your avatar; and Miner's Haven, which also offered a new virtual item for your avatar.

These are all highly successful tycoon games with visits well into the millions. However, with Roblox fans constantly working to create new and better games, you never know which tycoon will end up at the top later on!

CHAPTER 13
Getting Gifts

Roblox offers gifts as well as promotional and contest items. Gifts are usually placed on sale in the catalog and coincide with a specific time of year or event. Sometimes Roblox hands out gifts to players for winning a contest or doing something specific. To both Roblox players and creators alike, gifts are special items that are opened after a period of time to reveal a surprise. This could mean that a gift is no longer being given or sold but still hasn't been opened.

COLLECTIBLE GIFTS

There are also special gifts that are given as collectibles multiple times, such as the following.

TELAMON'S MYSTERY BOX

This gift was issued by Telamon Chaos Institute, and if you owned it you received either the Blue Banded Top Hat, Mystery Donuts, the Blame John Tie, Telamon's Chicken Suit (free), Telamon's Crafting Jewel (free), or LOLWUT (free), depending on the date you owned it.

BRIGHTEYES' TREASURE CHEST

This gift is also classified as an accessory in the Comedy genre. Depending on the dates you owned it and the box number, you received Brighteyes' Lavender Egg of Anticipation (or Pink), Brighteyes' Bloxy Cola Hat (free), O RLY owl, Brighteyes' Halloween Leftovers, McBrighteyes Shamrockin' Headphones, or Kilty McJig's 8-Bit Fedora.

REESE'S MYSTERY PONY PIÑATA

This gift's contents are considered a "quantum paradox, which may or may not exist at any given time." Depending on the date, LOLHOW Apple or a Magical Rainbow Pony has fallen out of the piñata.

Unfortunately, there isn't a particular schedule to determine when you might get one of these gifts or when there will be a new gift. Once an item has been given, the box, chest, or piñata will update the descriptions and the prize will no longer be distributed.

SPECIAL PROMOTIONS AND CONTEST ITEMS

You can also get gifts during special promotions and contests on Roblox. These items are distributed as gifts during holidays, as awards for certain activities during special events, as gifts for a Roblox contest prize, or in a special promotion for purchasing a Roblox game card. These items might also end up on sale in the catalog.

Roblox has a trading system that allows members of Builders Club to exchange Limited and Limited U items, as well as Robux, with other members. In order to use this system, you and anyone you trade with must have this feature enabled on the Privacy tab of your Account Settings page.

First you will go to the other player's profile page. If you need to find the player, you can enter their name into the top search bar of the website. When you find their profile page, select the button that looks like three dots at the top right corner of their username and Friends/Followers boxes. On the pop-up menu you can select Trade Items.

You should then see a window with all the items that you and the other player have to trade. When you hover your mouse over each item, you will see either Add to Offer button, which is for your items, or Request, which is for their items. In some cases you might want to make your trade offer more attractive by including additional Robux. However, there is a 30 percent transaction fee if the offer is accepted. Further, the number of Robux can't be more than 50 percent of the current offer calculated after subtracting the transaction fee.

When you have created the trade you want, you can submit it, which will send the new trade information to the player in a private message.

You might also want to keep track of current or past trades. You can view a list of pending inbound and outbound trades, completed trades, and inactive trade offers on your Trade Type pull-down menu on the Trade page.

You should keep in mind that you don't have to accept any trade offers you get (and your trade offers might not be accepted as well). When you get the trade request, you will have the option to accept, decline, or counter. If you don't want to accept the current offer and want to change it by requesting more items or Robux, you can select Counter to see if the other player will agree to the offer.

DONATING AND ACCEPTING DONATIONS

You can also make donations to help other players out, or you can accept donations from players who wish to help you. There isn't a way to gift items right now, but you can give currency to another account through the donation system. This means that you purchase an item like a T-shirt, often referred to as a Donation T-shirt, or pants from a player who has Builders Club. You do need to be a member to sell items and receive donations. Neither Builderman nor Roblox is able to donate to players.

CHAPTER 15

Becoming a Member of Builders Club

Although you can certainly play Roblox for free, you can also become a member of Roblox clubs and get access to additional perks and features that you won't find in the free version. These clubs are considered premium service and, depending on how active you are in the game, could be worth the monthly or annual fee.

Extra features you will find once you become a member of Builders Club include more places to build, daily Robux, access to trading and sales features so you can earn more Robux, and even opportunities to participate in Roblox's DevEx program. Roblox considers members of Builders Club to be an integral part of the future development of the platform. According to Roblox, membership dues are used to further develop new features and advancements for everyone on Roblox to enjoy.

AN EXPLANATION OF THE BENEFITS AND PERKS OF BUILDERS CLUB MEMBERSHIP

To get a better idea of what the Builders Club membership is worth, you might need a short explanation of what some of the perks actually are. These features are also covered in more detail in other chapters. However, here is a brief explanation of the membership perks you get with Builders Club.

DAILY ROBUX

Robux and how to use the Roblox currency is explained in more detail in Chapter 8, but for Builders Club membership it's important to know that it means you get daily Robux just for being a member. The amount you get each day is dependent on your membership level, but you don't have to do anything else to get the extra Robux in your account every day. You can use your Robux to buy outfits for your characters and lots of other extra features.

ACTIVE PLACES

Your membership will also provide more opportunities for active places that you can

go to and play games. This ranges from 10 active places in the Classic level to 100 in the Outrageous level.

JOIN GROUPS

You can also join groups with your membership, from 10 groups as a Classic member to 100 as an Outrageous member.

CREATE GROUPS

As a Builders Club member you can also create groups. Classic members can create 10, Turbo members can create 20, and Outrageous members can create up to 100 groups. If you have the free membership, you can only create five groups.

SIGNING BONUS

All three levels currently give you $100 Robux as a signing bonus, but it's only for first-time memberships.

PAID ACCESS

This feature allows members 70 percent paid access to the game, as opposed to free membership, which gives you only 10 percent paid access.

NO EXTERNAL ADS

This privilege simply means you don't have to see any banners or ads while you're on the main website if you're a Builders Club member.

SELL ITEMS

The privilege of selling items is exclusive to those who are Builders Club members.

VIRTUAL HAT

Members get a virtual hat, which you don't get if you have a free membership. This hat can go along with any character or outfit and basically lets other players know that you're a member of Roblox Builders Club.

BONUS GEAR

You also get cool extra gear with your membership. This gear not only looks good but can also help you fight off enemies, and can help in other ways, depending on the gear. Nonpaying members do not have access to this bonus gear at all.

BC BETA FEATURES

If you like being the first to try out new features, you'll like the ability to get access to BC Beta Features before others.

ACCESS PERSONAL SERVERS

Some members consider access to personal servers an opportunity to have more fun in Roblox. Again, this is only available to members of Builders Club.

TRADE SYSTEM

The trade system is also exclusive to Builders Club members.

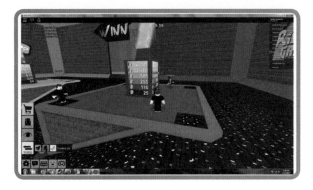

BUILDERS CLUB MEMBERSHIP LEVELS

The levels of Builders Club, the cost, and some of the extra features you get with each level include the following.

CLASSIC BUILDERS CLUB

For the Classic level of Builders Club, you get 10 places on your account instead of one, and you can join and create 10 groups as opposed to the basic version, which only allows you to join five groups. You also earn a daily income of 15 Robux, and you can sell your creations to other players in the Roblox catalog. As a Builders Club member, you also get the ability to browse the site without external ads, and you earn the Builders Club construction hat. The Classic version of Builders Club typically costs about $5.95 per month, or $57.95 annually. This level, along with the Turbo and Outrageous levels, also earns a signing bonus of $100 Robux (R$100).

TURBO BUILDERS CLUB

Turbo Builders Club includes all the benefits of the classic version, with the addition of a few more upgrades. For instance, you get 25 places instead of 10, plus a daily income of 35 Robux. Like the Classic version of Builders Club, you get the opportunity to sell your creations to others through the Roblox Catalog, and you can browse the site without external ads. You also get the Turbo Builders Club red site manager's hat and an exclusive gear item. This level of the club usually costs about $11.95 per month, or $85.95 annually.

OUTRAGEOUS BUILDERS CLUB

The top level of Builders Club, the Outrageous Builders Club, gives you the most perks and features out of all the levels of membership. This level costs about $19.95 per month, or $129.95 annually, and offers 60 daily Robux, 100 places, 100 groups, and the Outrageous website theme, as well as many other benefits.

HOW TO PURCHASE A MONTHLY SUBSCRIPTION OF BUILDERS CLUB

All memberships automatically renew if you purchase them directly from the site, but you can cancel before the renewal date if you decide to do so. It's important to note that these memberships are also nonrefundable. You can also purchase monthly memberships of Builders Club through the mobile apps on iTunes, Google Play, and Amazon.

If you purchase your membership through iTunes, Amazon, or Google Play, you should keep your receipt in case you need it in the future to verify account ownership. In order to purchase membership through one of the apps, you typically need to select the Builders Club icon, choose the membership level you want, and then confirm your purchase. You cannot purchase recurring memberships through mobile apps – only directly from the Roblox website. However, you can purchase one- or three-month memberships of any of the Builders Club levels with your mobile device.

At the end of 2015, the sale of electronic gift cards through the Roblox site was discontinued, although you can still use and redeem them if you have them. You can still purchase and gift electronic game cards for Roblox at retailers like Walmart, Target, GameStop, Best Buy, Toys"R"Us, 7-Eleven, and EB Games. You can use Roblox Cards for bonus gear hats, Builders Club subscriptions, and other Roblox expenses you might encounter.

SIX-MONTH AND LIFETIME BUILDERS CLUB MEMBERSHIPS

At one time there were options for six-month recurring and lifetime memberships, but as of August 2015 these options are no longer available. However, if you already had one of these memberships, you were essentially grandfathered in and were able to keep your membership until you decide to cancel.

CANCELING BUILDERS CLUB MEMBERSHIP

You do have the option to cancel your membership at any time. You can turn off auto-renewal before your renewal date, and you will be able to take advantage of your Builders Club privileges for the rest of the period you paid for. Simply select Cancel Membership Renewal when you go to the Billing tab on your Settings page to confirm your cancellation.

As with most games, it's up to you to decide whether or not you need to chat. It does come in handy, however, if you like to meet new players and interact with your friends while you play. Whether you use this feature or not, here's what you should know.

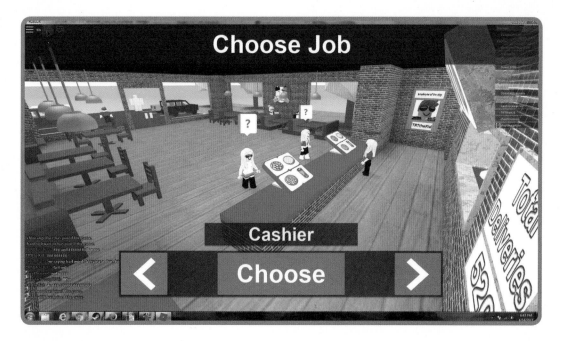

The Roblox in-game chat feature is restricted according to the account's privacy mode or filter. To start chatting you simply press the / key on your keyboard, which will open a chat window and a chat bar where you can type what you want to say, then hit the Enter key to send your message. When you click on the chat icon at the top left of your screen, you can also pull up the chat window and chat bar.

Because Roblox wants to make sure developers and players of all ages are safe, you and your parents should review the many privacy settings and age-appropriate chat modes that Roblox offers. To ensure that you're using the settings and modes that are best for you, we have included some additional information on chat and privacy.

Posts and chats of players who are age 12 and younger are filtered according to appropriate content and behavior and to prevent any personally identifiable information from being posted. Players age 13 and older have the ability to use more words and phrases than those who are younger, but inappropriate chat and sharing personal information is still restricted. These filters cover all areas of Roblox communication. When it comes to the ability to chat, all accounts both under and over the age of 13 can limit or completely disable who can chat with them on the site or in-game, who can send messages, and who can

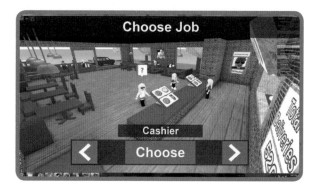

If you want to disable in-game chat, you simply log in to your account, go to your Account Settings page by clicking the gear icon at the top right, and then click the Privacy tab. Select No One under "Who can chat with me in game?" Make sure you save your settings by scrolling to the bottom and clicking Save.

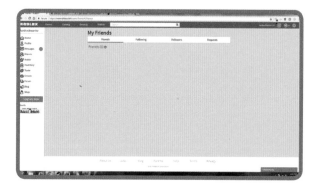

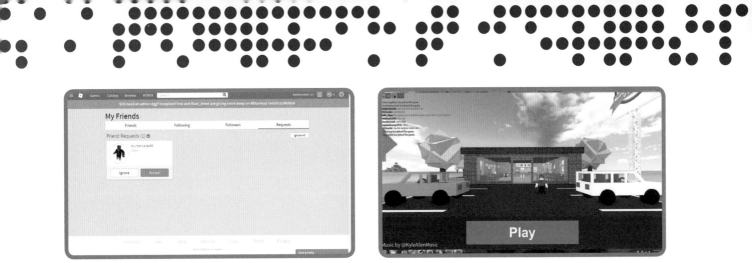

follow them into games or invite them to VIP Servers. If you are age 12 or younger, you can select either Friends or No One.

Further, all accounts have the option to enable a Parent Pin, which requires a four-digit code to make any changes to an account. These settings can be found in the Security and Privacy Tabs of the Account Settings page.

If at any time, through chat or any other method of communication, there is harassment, bullying, or spamming, regardless of age, you can block the user and report the account to Roblox for removal.

CHATTING ON MOBILE

If you choose to chat with your friends, you can also chat from a mobile device. To do this, you, of course, need the Roblox Mobile App. First, select a game. To send your own message, you will need to tap the message icon at the top left of the screen. The pop-up keyboard will allow you to enter your message and then tap Return, which might look like an arrow pointing to the left on the far right of the keyboard.

You can also disable in-game chat from your mobile device by logging in to the account, going to Account Settings, and tapping More in the lower right corner, followed by Settings. The pull-down menu will include Privacy, where you will find "Who can chat with me in game?" Here you will want to select No One and then save.

CHAPTER 17
Making New Games, Trees, and Doors: Building Anything You Want

In order to make a new game, you first need to create the level. Open Roblox Studio if it has already been installed. If not, you can find the download link on the Roblox.com/Develop page. When you open Roblox Studio, you should see the welcome page with options to create new games, open existing games, or browse Wiki articles.

Select Create a New Game and choose one of the Game Templates, depending on your preference. You can choose from the Basic templates, which are empty games, Theme templates, which include pre-built games based on settings, or Gameplay templates, which include built-in custom gameplay.

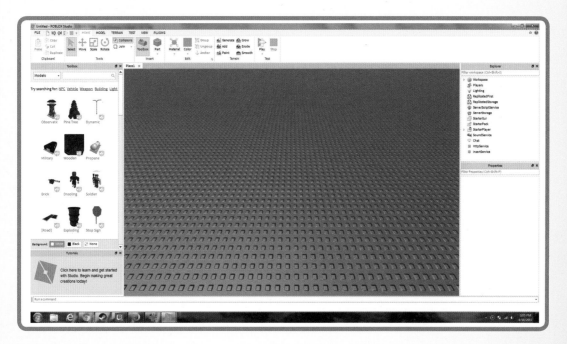

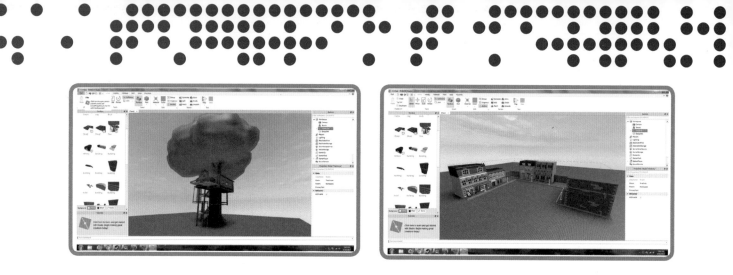

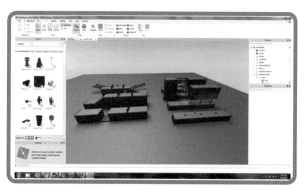

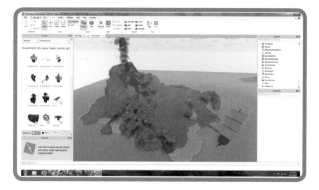

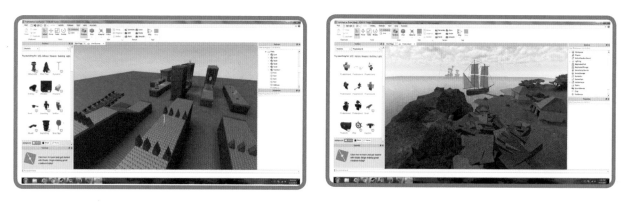

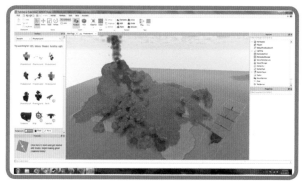

It's also important to understand how the camera controls work. The Roblox Studio camera is free-floating, meaning it can move anywhere you need or want it to. If you right-click and drag your mouse in the 3D view, you can rotate the camera in place. Use the scroll wheel to zoom the camera in and out, and use key commands for other actions. For example, the W and S buttons move forward and backward, and the A and D keys move side to side. If you want to move the camera up and down use the E and Q keys. Hold down the Shift key while you move the camera to move more slowly. The comma and period keys will rotate the camera in place, and you can use the Page Up and Page Down keys to pitch the camera up and down.

FOCUSING THE CAMERA

You might also want to focus the camera on objects in the 3D view. After you click on Part

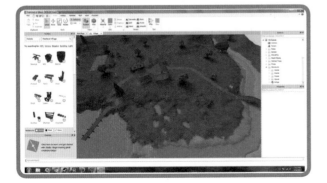

or Model, you can press the F key to focus the camera on your selection and snap the camera in for a closer look. Use rotation controls such as the comma or period, and Page Up or Page Down to rotate around your selection. Use one of the movement keys – W, A, S, D, Q, or E – to exit the focus mode.

CREATE NEW PARTS

To build a new game, you will need to create new parts. Click the Part button to insert a new part into your game, and select the arrow below the Part button to insert a Part, Sphere, Wedge, or Cylinder. You can move parts by clicking on them and dragging them around. Change how the part looks with the Scale, Color, and Material tools. The Move tool will let you move a part along an axis by dragging on the arrow; Rotate allows you to rotate a selected part by dragging the circular handles. With the Scale tool, you can resize a selected part by dragging the handles as well. You can change the color of a part by clicking the part and then Color, and if you want to change the material, click the part and then the Material tool.

USING YOUR TOOLBOX

The Toolbox holds Models and Decals created by other Roblox members that are free and can help you build your games. If you click an asset in the Toolbox, you will be able to insert it into your game. The models that are marked "High Quality" have been checked by Roblox and have been determined to work straight out of the toolbox.

PLAY YOUR GAME

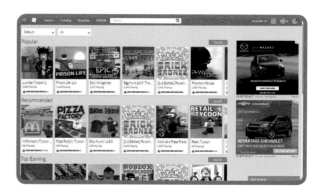

You can play your game right inside Studio, which is a good idea anyway to ensure it works properly. Once you press the Play button, your character will be inserted into the game. If you want to make changes when you're done playing, you can press Stop to undo any changes you made while playing the game.

As always, it's recommended that you frequently save your work while you're building your game. This saves your progress on the Roblox servers and prevents you from accidentally losing all your hard work. To save in Studio, press File and then Publish to Roblox As, and click one of the slots to save. You can also save by clicking on one of your existing save slots, which will overwrite the game that you currently have saved there. There is no limit to the number of save slots you use on Roblox.

GET CREATIVE: HOW TO MAKE A TREE

Once you get going in Roblox, you might be inspired to get creative and build other items, such as trees. We've included some very basic and easy instructions for creating your first tree – and it's easier than you might think.

First, insert a Part to use as your trunk and then select the Part button on the Home tab. Use the Scale tool to make the part narrow and tall. Next, use the sphere to create the leaves for the top of the tree: click on the arrow under the Part button and select Sphere. You can use the Scale tool to drag the green handle and make the sphere larger. Now you can move the sphere to the top of the trunk part you first made. If you have trouble dragging your sphere, you can also use the Move tool.

While this allows you to create a tree shape, you might still want to add some color and make the parts a better material. To color the trunk, first click on the shape, then click on the arrow under the Color tool and select one of the brown colors of your choice. To make the trunk a texture that appears wooden, you would do the same with the Material tool and select Wood.

Next, you can choose the material Grass and the color green from the Color tool to change the color and material of the top of your tree. And there you have it! You should have something that resembles a tree.

Keep in mind that when you're playing a game with this type of tree, the top part will be easy for a character to push . If you want to make sure it doesn't move at all, you can select the sphere shape and click on the Anchor button to make sure it won't move. You can also anchor the trunk of the tree if you want to be sure it doesn't move, either.

LET'S BUILD A CAMPFIRE

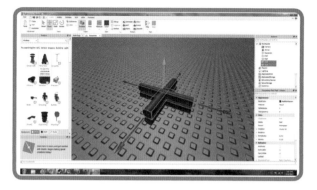

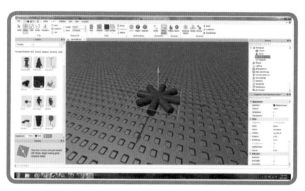

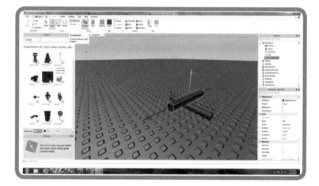

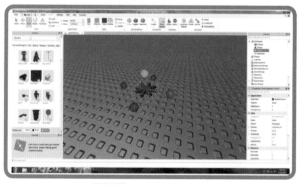

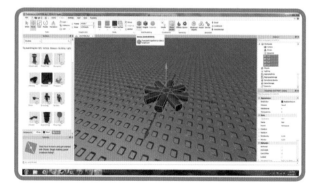

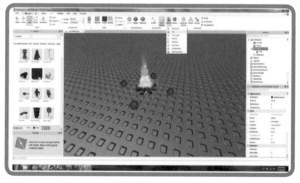

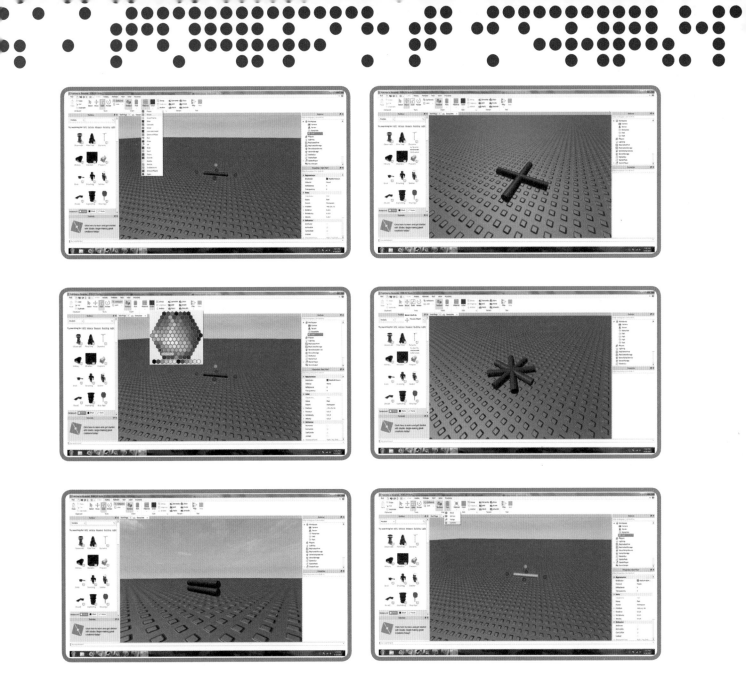

One of the most common creations in Roblox worlds is the campfire. Here's how you can build your own, using the Collisions toggle, particles, and custom lights, without worrying about actually catching anything on fire.

First, build the base out of thin parts, made by changing the FormFactor property of the

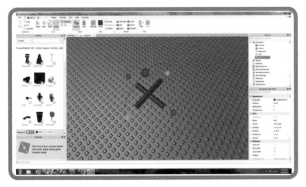

parts. Now you can add a part as the first log on the fire. Insert a new part for the log and anchor it. Next, rotate the log so it is sticking out of the base at an angle. Studio prevents parts from rotating or moving through other parts, but you can disable this by turning off the Collisions toggle. Rotate the log so it's angled and pointing toward the center.

Fortunately, you don't have to create each log individually. Copy the log you have created using the Duplicate button, then use the Rotate and Move tools to move the duplicated log. To add fire to your campfire, select the base part under the logs and click on the Model tab. You can then click Effects and select Fire. If the fire isn't big enough to cover your logs, you can enlarge it by opening the Explorer and Properties windows. Choose Fire from the Workspace and change the Size property of Fire to a large value, depending on how much you need to cover the logs.

Now you have a fire, but you don't yet have the illuminating effect around it. To create this effect, you can add a PointLight. Select the campfire base again and click on the Model tab; choose Effects and select PointLight. Now you can work on making the light brighter and the glow a color that actually looks like fire. Select PointLight from the Explorer window. Change Brightness to 10, Range to 15, and Color to Orange, and now you should have a realistic-looking and cozy campfire.

YOUR ENTRYWAY TO THE WORLD: MAKE A SWINGING DOOR

You can also make a door on Roblox, which you'll find is a fairly common structure in many of the games. Thanks to the Roblox physics engine, you can make all sorts of movable structures and contraptions with the use of joints.

First you need the frame of the door. You can use the Part tool to insert four parts, one for each part of the frame. The Scale tool will help you resize the parts according to the size you want your door to be.

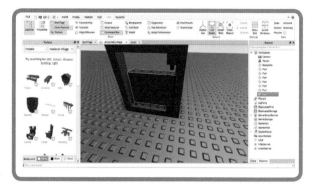

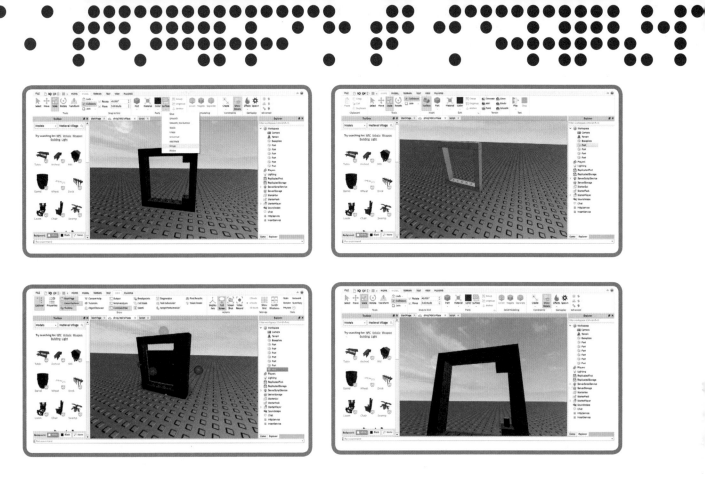

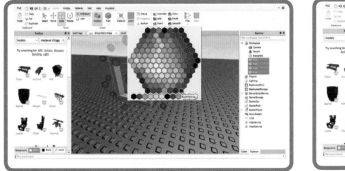

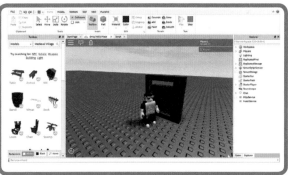

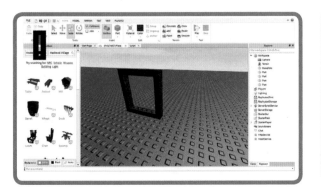

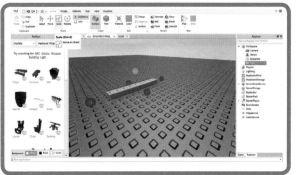

MAKING DOOR HINGES

Next you'll need hinges for your door, which is a special type of joint that allows rotation. For your first hinge, create a 1x1x1 part and place it at the bottom of your frame, one stud away from the edge of the frame. If you click on the Surface tool, you'll see a Hinge, where you can click on the top of the 1x1x1 part. At the top of the part, you'll see a small axle. For the top hinge, make another 1x1x1 part and place it at the top of your door, above the first hinge you made. Use the Surface tool to put the hinge on the bottom of the new part. If you run into problems dragging small parts like this, you can try to use the Move tool instead.

MAKING THE DOOR

Now we can make the door for the frame and hinges. First, create a new part and scale it to fit the frame you've created. However, it shouldn't completely fill the frame or you won't be able to open the door. Now you can try playing your game to see if the door swings open and closed. You will likely see gaps in the door, but those are needed for it to swing open. They don't have to be wide, though. You can use the 1/5th Stud radio button to drag or scale parts .2 studs at a time instead of one.

If you click this button and use the Scale tool, you can stretch the sides of the door so the gaps aren't quite so wide.

You might also want to use the Scale tool to make the hinge parts thinner and to make sure part of the door touches the top and bottom hinges. Based on your preferences, you can now also change the color and material of the door and its frame by using the Color and Material buttons.

MOVING THINGS WITH CONVEYOR BELTS

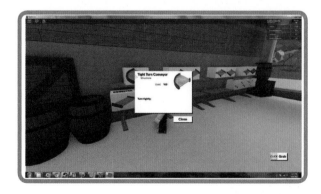

You can create and use conveyor belts in Roblox to move objects. It might seem like a complicated project, but conveyor belts in Roblox are actually pretty simple. Your first step is to insert a new part, and then you'll use the Scale tool to get the part to the size you want. Next, you will use the Surface tool to make the top area of the part Smooth. Finally, select the part and click on Anchor to anchor it down. If you skip the anchoring step, your conveyor belt will not work.

To make parts move across the top, you need to change the velocity in Properties. For unanchored parts, velocity will make the part move, but, for anchored parts, velocity makes anything that touches the part move.

Determine the direction you want the parts to move. In Roblox, the X, Y, Z system is used for positions and velocities of the parts. If you move the part around, you will see the Position property change. If you move the parts horizontally, it will move them in the X or Z

direction. Up and down, however, moves it in the Y direction.

You will see a four-stud grid overlaid on the baseplate, with three arrows at the center to indicate the axes. The corner is the Origin. Move your part near the arrows to determine the direction of the velocity. Next, click the View tab and then Properties. In the window, you will see Velocity. Click the arrow beside Velocity to change the values. If you move a part in Studio, the velocity will reset. If you move a conveyor, it is important to make sure you reset the property under Velocity.

Now you can press Play and step on the part to see if the character moves on the conveyor. If you want to fool around with changing how the conveyor moves, you can apply velocity to both X and Z to go diagonally, or you can set the Y velocity to throw both parts and players up when they touch it. This is also how you create springboards and trampolines.

KEEP OUT: RESTRICTED DOORS

Restricted doors, or VIP doors, restrict access to certain areas to certain users. Although creating a restricted door is a little more complicated than other structures, once you have the door created, you shouldn't have much difficulty.

Some of the most common restrictions for doors include being a certain player, owning a certain asset, such as a T-shirt, badge, or hat, or being in a specific group. You could also be a creator of the place or a good friend of a certain player or creator.

However, you don't want to just make restricted doors carelessly. It's recommended that you think carefully before creating restricted doors or restricting access to a particular area. One of the problems is that restricted doors can become overused when they're used to protect rooms with certain items. Instead, you could give the items to players rather than having them enter the room when they die.

If you can't avoid creating a restricted door, here's how to make one. First, create the door and make it the size of a character, typically 4x5x1, so players can get through it. Also, you should anchor the door so it doesn't move when players touch it. You won't be able to get the exact dimensions with the Brick Form-Factor, so you'll want to change the FormFactor to Symmetric. Otherwise, you could also make the door a little bigger than a character; as long as a character can fit through it, you shouldn't have a problem.

Next, go to the Insert menu and choose Object. Use the dialog that appears to insert script in the door and then open it to edit in Script Editor. Define the variable that contains a reference to it, such as the variable "door." To make the door open and close, you need another function. You will need to use a loop to make the door fade so that it disappears. Use the Transparency property to change the opacity and then change the door's CanCollide property to allow players to walk through it. Use the Touched event so that the door opens when a character touches it. Then you'll need to check if the player meets any of the restrictions of the door.

The restrictions will be under Boolean expressions. If any are true, the door will open, wait four seconds, and then close. Some of the common restrictions you can use include designating a certain player by checking that the player's name is equal to a certain string and matches. This looks something like the following:

player.Name == "PlayerName"

Another restriction is being in a certain group. You can check if the player is a member of a certain group by using IsInGroup, which uses the group's ID. If the player is in the group ID, they will be able to enter through the restricted door. If not, they will not. An example would look like:

player:IsInGroup(5648)

You can also restrict according to whether or not the player owns a certain asset, such as a certain badge, by using UserHasBadge. This method can apply to hats, gear, T-shirts, pants, and even places. The UserHasBadge uses userID and badgeID. The userID matches the ID of a player, and the badgeID matches the ID of a particular asset.

Restricted doors can also be used for the player who is the creator of the place, using the player's name with a predefined name such as the place's owner's name. It uses CreatorID and compares it to the player's ID, and will work in any place. It looks something like this:

game.CreatorId == player.userId

Also, if you're a friend of a certain user, you could use IsFriendsWith as the userID if, for instance, you want to allow all the friends of a creator.

After you've mastered creating a door and restricting access, you could take it further and make the door do things like kill, for example, if the player is not allowed through. For some players, this makes the restricted door more secure and prevents restricted players from getting through because someone else opened the door for him.

MAKING A RIVER USING TERRAIN TOOLS

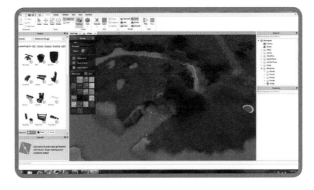

Do you want to include some nature or landscapes in your Roblox world? Well, good news: you can use the Terrain tool to create any natural surrounding you want. Here's a brief guide to creating a river using these tools.

First, move the camera in Studio so you can look straight down at the world, kind of like you're looking down from the sky. Next, press the Add button on the Home tab. Your cursor will change to a large blue circle, and you'll see a new menu on the left. You can select the kind of terrain you want from this menu. If you want to start by adding grass, this is the default for the Terrain tool. Click and drag in the 3D view, and you will see grass growing under your cursor. You can keep adding grass until you have a large area filled in.

Now that you have your grassy area, you can add water for the river. Click on the Paint button and select the Water material. Click and drag a line across the grass to change it to water; you'll see that it's already starting to look like a river. To add a small strip of sand on either side of your newly created river, change your paint material to Sand and make your brush smaller by dragging the slider to the left. You can now click and drag your cursor over the grass on both sides of your river to change it to sand.

Now you have a grassy area, sand, and a river in your game. You can experiment with the Terrain tools to create hills next to the river. Use the Grow button to form a hill. You can change the size by shrinking it with the Erode button or smoothing out the corners with the Smooth button, depending on how you want the hill to look.

You can also use these tools and the Generate button to make a large region of terrain quickly without going through the process to add it manually. This will generate a landscape for you so that you only have to configure it by moving the sliders according to how you want it to look. The Terrain Generator can be found in Roblox Studio and generates a combination of different BaseParts to create terrains and

landforms. It can build up to 2,048 cells in each direction.

Terrain tools like the Smooth Terrain feature allow you to change how your world looks, with the addition of natural features like beaches and mountains. With this feature, you can make grass, sand, brick, and rock according to the textures of your choice, resulting in more realistic-looking landscapes. Plus, you can use Smooth Terrain to convert old terrain you've already created by simply clicking a button. When you switch to Smooth Terrain, you also get extra tools that can help you create your natural environments faster and more easily.

If you want to give it a try, you can find the Smooth Terrain tool under the Terrain tab in Roblox Studio. When you click the Convert to Smooth button, you'll see the change to your landscape.

WE NEED SOME WHEELS

Now, your character needs some way to get around town, right? Let's make a car. Once you get the hang of making your first basic vehicle, you can start to build more detailed cars for your world. Your basic car only needs a seat, body, and wheels, so let's get started!

First you'll need to insert a new part to be used as the main body of the car. Use the Scale tool to make it as long and as tall as you like. Add a Cylinder for the first wheel. With the Surface tool, you can make one of the sides of a hinge. Place the cylinder right next to the car body so the wheel doesn't fall off.

Duplicate the wheel so you have four wheels for your vehicle.

Using the Rotate tool, make sure the hinge of the wheel faces the body that you first made. You can raise the body using the Move tool so it's off the ground. Next, create your VehicleSeat, where the player will sit to drive. Right-click in the 3D view, over Insert Object and then click VehicleSeat. Move the Vehi-cleSeat to the top of the body. Now you can press the Play button and place your character on the VehicleSeat, and you're off to your next destination!

Other vehicles you might be interested in creating and navigating on Roblox include planes, skateboards, and Hyperbikes. Here is some more information on navigating differ-ent types of vehicles.

For cars, you can choose from either the vehicle seat type that we just covered or the tool-based kind. You can drive vehicle seat types in the same way as walking, with the W, A, S, and D keys on your keyboard. Tool-based cards are controlled a little differently. For the most part, the Y key can start the engine of a car and the X key stops it. You can click left or right to turn the car in the direction you want. Special controls like the T key can flip the car.

Planes are tool-based and can be controlled with keys as well. The Y key starts the plane engine, the X key stops the plane, and the G key closes the hatch. You can turn planes right or left, and they can also come equipped with bombs and guns. The F key fires primary guns, the B key drops bombs, and the E key fires secondary guns. Believe it or not, there are also special keys for planes. The C key turns an invisibility cloak on and off, the G key does a barrel roll, and the R key gives the player landing gear.

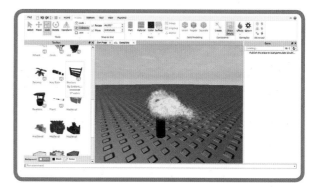

Unfortunately, many of the vehicles on Roblox don't actually work and are published only to troll the player who takes them. Further, Roblox updates have stopped many vehicles from working.

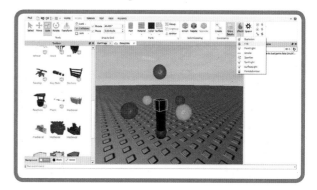

GETTING STARTED MAKING BUILDINGS

By now you've figured out how to make a bunch of new stuff in Roblox. This time, we're going to create a basic office building. You can use this guideline to then make any type of building you like.

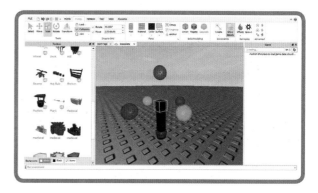

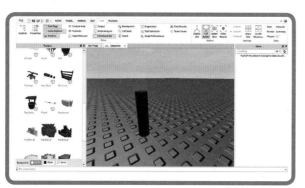

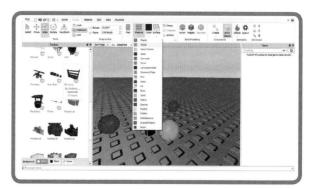

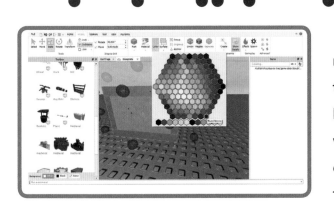

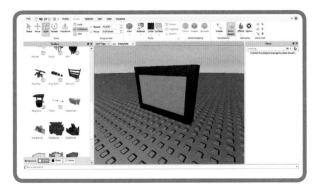

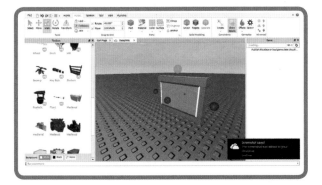

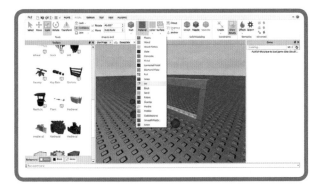

First, you need a single window. You'll need to insert new parts into your game using the Part button. Two of the three parts will be the window frame, and the last will be the window pane or the glass. You can change the color and the material of the parts according to how you want each part to look.

For glass, you probably want it to be clear so you can see through it like a normal window. Open Properties and click on the Glass part. Select the property Transparency and set it to 0.5. Although your building will need more windows, you don't have to create one at a time. Instead, you can copy the one you created. Click and drag to select all of the parts of the window and then use the Copy and Paste buttons to copy it. Place the copy next to the original window. The Duplicate button can also copy your window so you don't have to make each one from scratch. This is handy when you need a bunch of the same structure at once.

Paste your windows and then arrange them in a straight line. When you select the row of windows, you can copy and paste again and place it above the first row. You can keep repeating these steps until you have several rows stacked for the wall of the office building. Next you'll need to select your stack of

windows and copy and paste. Then, using your Rotate tool, you can rotate it 90 degrees and move the copy so that it fits next to your first stack of windows. Select both stacks, copy and paste, and rotate 90 degrees again. Move the copy so it fits next to the other stacks. The windows you've created should now form a four-sided structure.

Finally, insert a new part and use the Scale tool to cover the top of the building, and you now have a nice new office building to be proud of.

WORKING WITH MOTORS: MAKING A WINDMILL

In Roblox, you can also make things with motors that actually move. In this example, we'll go over how to make a windmill that moves. First, insert a new part, which will be the pole of the windmill, and use the Scale tool to make the pole narrow and tall. Next, add a part to use as the shaft of the windmill. This part should be small, and square like a box. Use the Move tool to keep this part suspended in midair until it's moved next to the top of the pole.

Next, select the Surface tool and choose Motor. Click on one of the sides of the shaft. You should see a small axle sticking out of the side of the part. The motor is what will make the windmill turn. Now you can move the part next to the pole so that the axle of the motor goes into the pole. Select the Surface tool and add Weld. Click the four outer sides of the shaft. The welds will hold the vanes in place. Insert another part and, using the Scale tool, make it long and thin, then place this part on top of the shaft. This is the first vane of the windmill.

Now you can copy and paste the vane and move the copy under the shaft. After you copy and paste again for another vane, use the Rotate tool to put this vane on its side, then use the Move tool to move it to the side of the shaft. Repeat this process for the other side of the windmill. Now the windmill should rotate if you press the Play or the Run button.

CHAPTER 18
Everything You Need for Your Tools and Meshes

There are lots of features you'll want to become familiar with when you start playing or creating with Roblox, some of which include tools and meshes.

Tools can be used to implement weapons, tools, and other objects in the game. In most cases, a tool in Roblox is a container like a model. To get started creating a new tool, right-click in the Workspace, choose Insert Object, and then choose Tool.

3D VIEW AND PICKING UP THE TOOL

Keep in mind that a tool is basically just a container, so it won't show up in your 3D view if there's nothing in it. If you right-click on the tool and insert a new part, the tool will show up in the 3D view. To pick up a tool, you need a part inside it called a Handle, so you'll need to rename the part in the tool to Handle. Now your character will be able to pick up the tool when you run your game.

You can have as many parts in your tool as you like, but make sure you only have one part called the Handle. This is the part that needs to attach to the character's hand so your tool can be carried. When you're building tools, you should make sure your parts are not anchored when you finish building. If any are anchored, you won't be able to move the tool and the character will get stuck when it tries to pick it up.

If you name more than one part the Handle, the tool will pick only one of the parts for the actual point where the character holds it. It's important that you don't use Surface welds when you're building your tool, otherwise your tools will fall apart when they're equipped. It's recommended that you instead change the Join behavior to Always and make sure the surfaces you select are either Smooth or SmoothNoOutlines.

While it's nice to have a handle on your tool for characters to hold, you don't have to have one. However, there won't be any visual representation in the 3D view. For a tool without a handle, you just turn off the RequiresHandle property of the tool you created.

WHAT IS EQUIPPING A TOOL?

You might now be wondering what it means to equip a tool. Tools can be equipped in a number of different ways, such as having the tool in the Workspace and then having a player collide with it. This gets the tool automatically added to the player's backpack. In this case, the tool automatically equips itself if the player doesn't already have anything equipped. However, this only works if the RequiresHandle property is set to True.

StarterPack is another way to give tools to players. When a player spawns, the contents of the StarterPack are copied into the player's backpack. This is one of the best ways to ensure that all players start with certain equipment.

Finally, you can use a script to give tools to players. However, this can be complicated, and you have to be careful when inserting a tool this way. If the player already has a tool equipped and you force another by using a script, both will be equipped and this can lead to problems.

DROPPING TOOLS

Eventually, you will want to drop a tool after you've been equipped with it. You can usually drop a tool by pressing the Backspace or Delete key if you are on OSX. You can also prevent this behavior if you change the behavior to false on the CanBeDropped setting of the tool. You can tell if a tool is in someone's backpack by looking at the bottom of their screen in an action bar.

UNDERSTANDING AND USING MESH

Meshes, or a MeshPart, are simulated mesh that can support the upload of custom meshes. A mesh is typically a 3D object that can be a hat, gear, or a part. Each one of these objects is made up of at least one mesh. There are different types of meshes, including SpecialMeshes, which contain BlockMeshes and Cylinder Meshes.

A BlockMesh is typically used to replace a part and has pointy edges. BlockMeshes are smooth instead of studded, welded, yielded, or glued. CylinderMeshes can change what a part looks like and are similar to and look identical to the SpecialMesh MeshType Cylinder.

Because of inappropriate content, the ability to place the mesh in a game was removed in 2011. However, in 2016 player meshes returned to Roblox Studio and a section was added to the Roblox Library. Users can create meshes without using exploits, but it's limited to fewer than 5,000 polygons. Although it can seem complex at first, if you're ready to dive into the world of meshes, this short guide can help get you started.

To add a mesh, you first need to insert a MeshPart by right-clicking in the Workspace and then selecting Insert Object. You can then select MeshPart from the menu, then insert a new part in the game with a placeholder mesh. Select the MeshPart and then find the MeshId property. If you want to insert a mesh from a file, click the Insert button next to the MeshId property to open a file dialog, where you can select the file you want to import. The file will be a local.fbx file.

If you already know the assetID of the mesh you want to use, you can enter it into the MeshId field. Note that you can only set the MeshId through the property panel in Studio.

You can insert mesh through the Game Explorer as well, if you prefer a different method. First make sure you've published your game and then right-click on Assets and Add Mesh in the Game Explorer panel. Once a mesh has been added to Game Explorer, you can insert a copy of the mesh into the game by double-clicking on it or by right-clicking and selecting Insert.

CHAPTER 19
Adding Sounds

Audio is important to any game, making it more fun and more entertaining. Adding sounds to your games might seem complicated, but once you do it a few times it will become easier.

You can upload custom .mp3 files to play in your games, and they can also be used by other developers. First, click on the Develop tab and select Audio on the left, then upload a local file and name it. Just be sure your file is an .mp3 or .ogg format and shorter than seven minutes. It will cost you to upload a sound, so make sure you choose wisely. The costs vary from 20 Robux up to 350, depending on the length of your sound.

You can also obtain sounds on Roblox through the Catalog. Once you purchase a sound, you can note the ID in the URL so you can load the sound into your game. Make sure you preload the sound so you can play it whenever you need it. First, add it to the Workspace, right-click on the object you want to be the parent in the Explorer, select Insert Basic Object and the sound, then set the SoundID property.

You can play sound just by using the Play function. The sound will play as soon as it's finished loading. Some of the sounds you might choose to play in your game include ambient sounds, which are played at a constant volume throughout a place and are used to add music, or 3D Sound, which is locational and used for sound effects. A sound is 3D if its parent is a part. These sounds have behaviors such as volume, stereo, and Doppler Effect.

ADDING MUSIC TO YOUR GAME

Have you been wondering how the games you play have these fun, catchy tunes playing during the game? Actually, you can add music to your game, and it's easy to do it. Many players and developers find that music helps give the game a professional appearance, creates a mood, and makes it more fun. Here are some brief instructions for adding music to your game.

First, to upload your music, you will need to upload a sound file for 100 Robux. These files can be up to 120 seconds long and can be

one of the songs already uploaded by Roblox developers in models, tools, and gear.

You can find music in the Catalog under a tab that lists all the audio that has been uploaded by users and administrators. Listen and preview the audio on the Audio page, and then put it in your inventory.

Next, you can go to the Configure page by clicking the gear icon and choosing Configure from the menu. Some of the options on this page include:

- Configuring the audio file's name
- Description for entering a summary of the file
- Turning comments on/off
- Adding a genre for classifying the audio so people can find it
- Making the sound free if you want the item to be freely available
- Adding a Version History so you can revert to an older version of the audio file

You can use audio files in places to add feeling and create mood. To add the audio to your place, first find the sound or upload it, get the asset ID, open Roblox Studio and a place in Edit Mode, open the Basic Objects panel, and double-click Sound. Next, open Properties, and next to SoundID enter "http://www.rob-lox.com/asset/?id=" plus the asset ID. Click on

StarterGUI and double-click LocalScript. Remove "print 'Hello world!'" and enter the following script: game.Workspace.Sound:Play(), then Publish to Roblox and save your game.

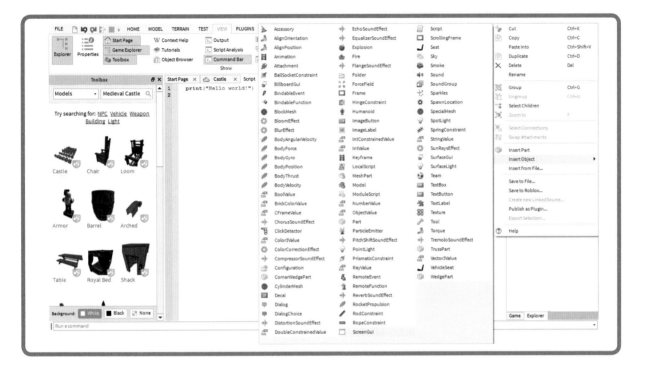

CHAPTER 20
Teleporters

By now you know that teleporters help you get around from one place to another. This allows you to go from place to place without closing a window. Here's a little bit more information regarding teleporting and enabling teleporters.

To set up a teleporter, you first need to open the Workspace. Next, open a teleporter model and select the placeID value in Properties. You will need to copy and paste the end of the link of the place you want to teleport to and insert it into the value. Then, copy and paste the spawn's name you want to teleport to into the DestinationSpawnName value. Finally, copy and paste the spawn's name you set up into the TeleporterName value in the teleporter's spawn. You can now enter the teleporter in online mode, where you'll be asked if you want to be teleported. You can select Yes and you will be sent to the place you set up the teleporter for.

Other reasons for teleporters include continuing to places or obstacle courses to decrease lag or any other inconvenience. Some things you should be aware of regarding teleportation:

- You cannot teleport to BC Only places if you are not a member of Builders Club.
- You cannot teleport into an inactive game.
- You cannot teleport into a Friends Only place if you are not a friend of the creator.
- There has been deceptive advertising involving the use of teleports to transport to unrelated places, usually an empty baseplate.
- Beware of bugs where players spawn as a Guest when they go into teleporters.

You might want to set up teams to play certain games with your friends and family members. Here's how you can add teams to your gameplay. Keep in mind that team names and colors, and the players on the team, can be viewed in-game on the leaderboard.

First, to enable teams, you need to select the Model tab and click Service in the Advanced section. Next, click Teams and then Insert. You will see a new object called Teams.

You can add team functionality to a Roblox game through its Team features. Once Teams are enabled, you can add a new team by right-clicking Teams and selecting Insert Object and Team. You can change the name of the team in the Properties window. First, select the team you want to change in the Explorer and then

check to see if Properties is open. Now you can change the name with the Name field and the color using the TeamColor field.

SPAWN LOCATIONS

Spawn Locations are usually Roblox objects that are closely tied to teams. Whenever a player joins a game or dies and respawns, the character will spawn at a SpawnLocation with the same TeamColor as the player's team. You can create a SpawnLocation when you click on the Model tab and then the Spawn button in the Gameplay section. In the Properties window, after you click on the SpawnLocation, you will see the TeamColor in the Teams section. It's important to note that this is different from the SpawnLocation's BrickColor, which is the displayed color of the part but has nothing to do with the team. Most players just make sure the SpawnLocation's BrickColor and TeamColor are different so no one is confused.

CHANGING AND AUTO-ASSIGNING TEAMS

You can change teams if you turn on AllowTeamChangeOnTouch on a SpawnLocation. If a player steps on that spawn, that player will join the team that was tied to that spawn. Roblox auto-assigns new players to a team. When a player joins a game with teams, the player will automatically go to the team with the fewest players. You can disable autojoin by selecting Team and opening the Properties window, where you can turn off AutoAssignable.

You can customize how your avatar moves with an animation package. Some of the bundles available in the Roblox Catalog include a Stylish Animation Pack, a Zombie Animation Pack, and a Levitation Animation Pack. These packs include special features for your avatar's movement. For example, you can fly with the Levitation Animation Pack. Each pack changes the way your avatar runs, walks, falls, jumps, swims, climbs, and idles, with plans to change others in the future.

To change and equip your avatar with an animation package, the process is a bit similar to dressing your avatar. First, go to the Avatar Editor page, where you'll see the Animations tab with a list of the animation packages you've acquired from the Catalog. Then, select the type of animation you want to change and choose the package. Each bundle varies in price, from 80 to 1,000 Robux, and is exclusive to the R15 avatar. There are plans to add more features and animation packages in the future.

CREATING ANIMATIONS

This also means you can create animations using the Animation Editor plugin in Roblox Studio. First you'll need to install the Animation Editor by logging in and installing the plugin. You can search Roblox Studio for the plugin by going to Tools, Manage Plugins, and Find Plugins. Search for Animation Editor and you should find it.

To edit a pose, you can click on the Animation Editor button in the toolbar. This is where you select the base of the object you want to define animations for and name it HumanoidRootPart. When you select the base part, the Editor window will open.

You will see a list of the parts in your model in a timeline where you can create a keyframe and define how the model should look.

Remember that each keyframe is a pose. When you run your animation, the parts will move between poses in the keyframes. To make a specific pose, simply drag the keyframe indicator to the timeline to define the pose, then click on the model at the point you want to manipulate. You can use the R key to go from rotating to moving. Each pose will create a keyframe in your timeline – you can create more than one pose for each of your keyframes. You also have the option to copy and paste poses into the editor by using the keys CTRL + while clicking on the pose. You can then move the indicator where you want it in the timeline, to be copied and pasted when you press CTRL-V.

PRIORITIZING ANIMATION

If you want to play an animation while another one is already running, such as making a jump animation and an animation when the character is standing still, you use priority to determine which animation to override. Animation priority consists of Core, which is the lowest priority, Idle, Movement, and then the highest priority, Action. Once you have set the priority, if you start an animation with a higher priority than one that is already playing, the new one with the higher priority will supersede the old animation.

PLAYING MORE THAN ONE ANIMATION AT A TIME

You might also want to play more than one animation at a time, rather than having one supersede the other. For this, you would need to make an animation in the Editor and select certain parts to include in the animation. The box beside the part name will designate whether or not you can include that part in the animation. When you play your animation, the excluded parts will continue the actions they were doing before the animation started.

CHANGING THE LENGTH OF YOUR ANIMATION

Click Edit and select Change Length. Your animation can be up to 30 seconds long. You can add or remove time using the cursor by clicking on the Edit button and selecting Add Time At Cursor/Remove Time At Cursor.

Once you've created your animation you can upload it to your places. Select File in the editor and then Export. This is where you create a new animation or overwrite one that already exists. Make sure you note the asset ID in the URL when you create it, because you will need it if you want to create an animation in a script.

If you want to import animations into the Editor to make changes, you can select the Import button under the File menu. This is where you'll need to enter the ID of the animation, which is the numerical part of the asset ID. You can only edit animations that you have created.

CHAPTER 23
Developer Exchange

You can earn money when you create games on Roblox through the Developer Exchange (DevEx) program. Once you've earned 100,000 Robux, you can even convert your Robux to real cash.

Besides agreeing to the DevEx Terms of Service, you also need to meet the following requirements to become part of the Developer Exchange.

- Member of the Outrageous Builders Club
- At least 100,000 earned Robux in your account
- Verified email address
- Valid DevEx portal account

- 13 years of age or older
- Community member in good standing

Once you meet all of these requirements, you can click the Cash Out button and follow the instructions to get your payment. If you're curious, the exchange rates for cashing out are as follows:

- R$100,000 for **$250 USD**

- R$250,000 for **$625 USD**

- R$500,000 for **$1,250 USD**

- R$1,000,000 for **$2,500 USD**

- R$2,000,000 for **$5,000 USD**

- R$5,000,000 for **$12,500 USD**

- R$8,000,000 for **$20,000 USD**

There is also a cash-out cap of $120,000 per year. As you can see, there's a great deal of potential to earn real money simply by creating great Roblox games. In fact, between October 2013 and January 2014, users earned $46,550 USD.

Developer Central can be found on the Develop page in the main navigation bar. This page is similar to the Build page, but instead includes features for developers such as metrics, special forums, toolkits, and tips. DevEx is one of the first features to become part of

Developer Central, and it's designed to give the Roblox community incentive to create more great games.

There are many success stories of developers who are able to make a living by playing and creating Roblox games – proof that it's much more than just an online video game. Once you get started navigating Roblox, it won't be long before you could be following in their footsteps and creating games that people love.

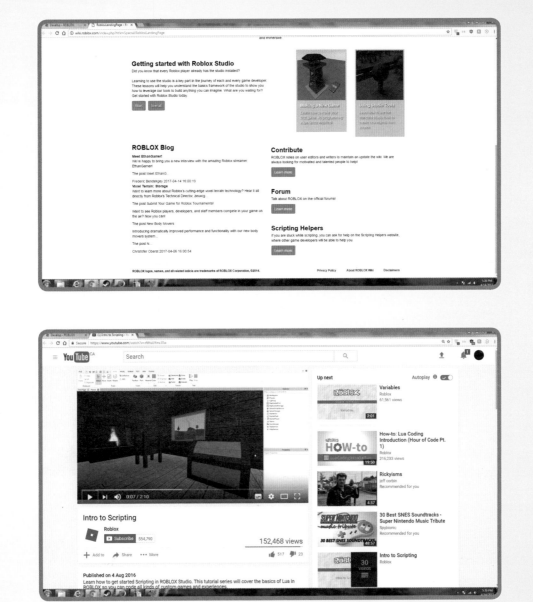

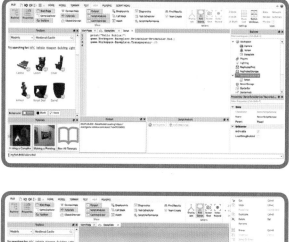

In order to get these instructions, you have to provide words the program understands. In Roblox, the language called Lua can be used in Roblox Studio to create games.

Click on the View tab and then open the Output and Command Bar panels to start. You will see the Command Bar at the bottom of Studio, where you can write instructions for the game. The Output window will show text responses as well as any mistakes.

One of the functions you'll want to become familiar with in scripting is the function called Print, which makes text appear in the Output window. First type the print ("Hello world!") and hit Enter in the Command Bar to get an idea of how it works. You should see what you typed in the Output panel with the instruction and the message. This means that the function Print will output whatever you include in the parentheses that follow.

In scripting, you might want to store information you can use later by using variables. These are kind of like boxes you can put information in. To create a variable you just need to give it a name and assign it a value. For example, you could use myFavoriteNumber = 6, which would store the number 6 into a variable called myFavoriteNumber. If you enter this into the output, you will notice that nothing will show because the Print function wasn't used.

Scripting in Roblox can get pretty in-depth and complicated, but we will include a brief introduction to get you started. Once you understand scripting, you're well on your way to creating anything you can imagine in your Roblox world.

First, scripts are a series of instructions that a program uses to create custom behavior.

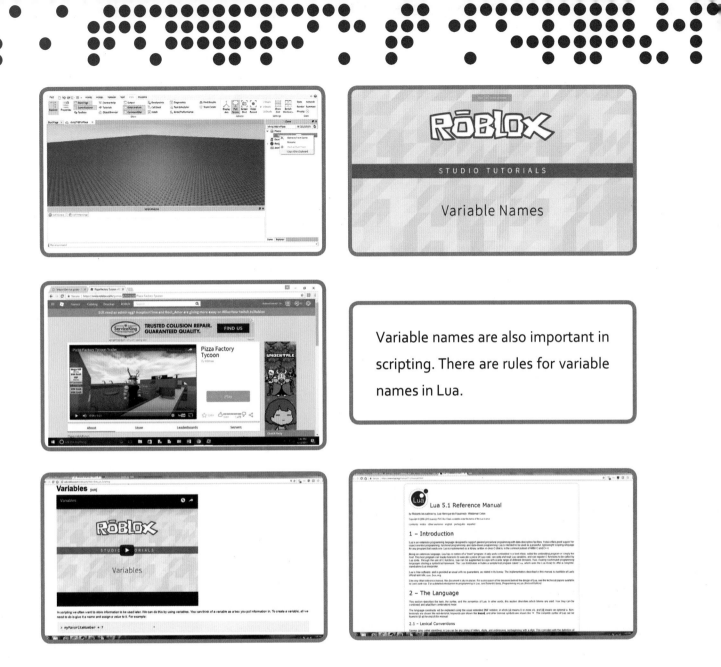

Variable names are also important in scripting. There are rules for variable names in Lua.

Some of these rules, for example, are guidelines such as that variable names can't have spaces in them, can't start with numbers, can't have special characters except for an underscore, can't be the same as any special words, such as "for," "and," "end," or "if," and can't be the same as functions, like Print.

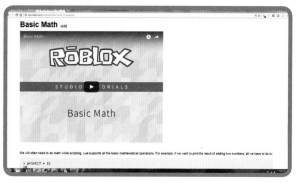

Scripting also includes basic mathematical operations. If you place a function like Print in front of it, you can guess that the mathematical operation will appear in the output box. While scripting involves many other functions and operations, these give you a basic understanding of where you'll start.

Here are some helpful resources for getting started with scripting – or if you run into any problems.

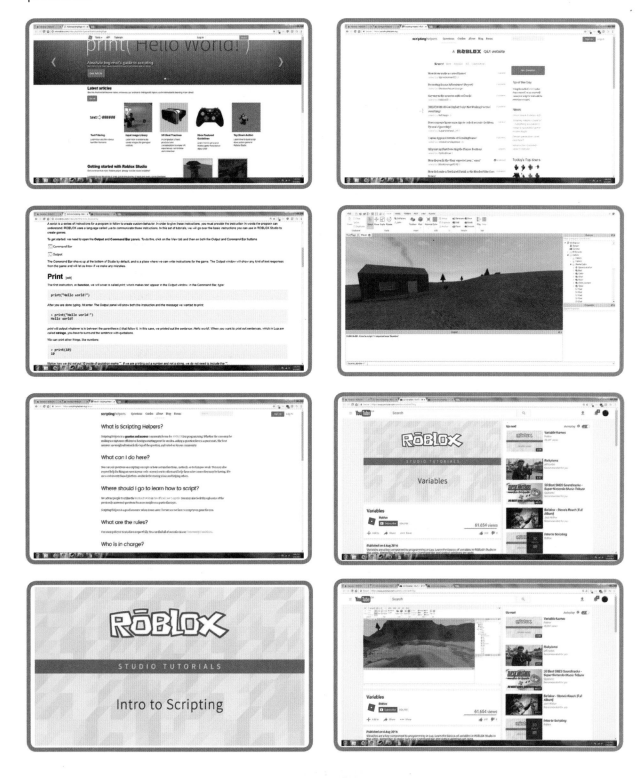

Understanding Graphical User Interface (GUI) can be complicated, especially if you're new to the world of creating with Roblox. Here's a short guide to help you out with the basics.

GUIs are 2D bits of image and text that appear on a player's screen. In Roblox, there are many different types of GUI you can use. To set up a GUI, you first need to put everything in a StarterGUI. This service is similar to the StarterPack, except that it's exclusive to GUIs. Whatever you put in the StarterGUI will be cloned into a player's PlayerGUI, which allows each player to view GUIs. Basically, if you want to create a picture that everyone can see, you simply insert it into the StarterGUI. In certain circumstances, such as when a player has died and is reset, the items in the PlayerGUI are removed and replaced, and the screen is reset.

Here's how to get started creating a GUI that covers the entire screen. First you'll need to open Roblox Studio and create a new place with a baseplate. Switch on Tools, Properties, and Explorer. In the Explorer panel, you'll need to select StarterGUI and click Insert in the toolbar, then click Object. Choose ScreenGUI from the box that pops up in the StarterGUI. Click Insert, Object, and then Frame, which is basically a rectangle that appears on your screen. Now, whenever a player enters, they should receive a copy.

EDITING

Now you can edit. In the Explorer, choose Frame, and you should see the properties in the Properties panel. In Properties, look for Size, which reads "{0, 0}, {0, 0}." Change these numbers to "{1, 0}, {1, 0}." Your screen should now be inside a gray frame, and you should no longer be able to see your screen properly. However, to test it, click Tools, Test, and Play Solo.

If you see the gray GUI covering your screen in test mode, you have successfully set up your first GUI.

Some other ScreenGUIs that are boxes that go on the screen include the following.

IMAGELABELS

These are similar to frames but allow you to display pictures on them. These are kind of like decals, which contain a property called Texture that shows the picture displayed, except that for ImageLabels it's called Image instead of Texture.

IMAGEBUTTONS

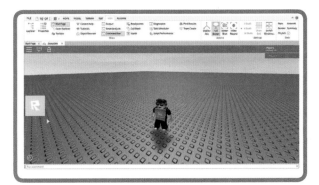

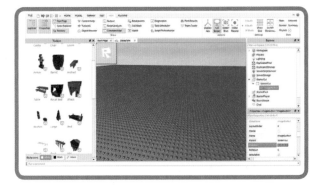

TEXTBOXES

You can use these with TextLabels and TextButtons. TextBoxes are unique in that you can type in them. They can be used for search engines, messaging, forums, or wherever you want a player to type.

3D SPACE GUIS

These are different from the others and don't go in a ScreenGUI. Instead, they go straight into the StarterPack. Many of them use a property called Adornee, which refers to the brick that it is attached to. There are two ways of setting it: using a script that automatically sets it or using a command bar to set it. Examples of 3D Space GUIs include the following.

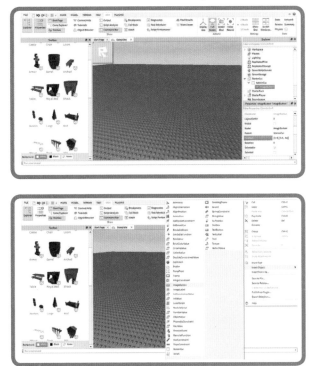

These are similar to ImageLabels except that you have to click on them to make them do anything. You can include script in an ImageButton to make specific actions occur.

TEXTLABELS

These don't have images but instead have text. All you have to do is make sure you edit the text properly, and you can display whatever text you want.

TEXTBUTTONS

Like TextLabels and ImageButtons, you can click on these, and you can include script like you can with ImageButtons.

HANDLES

These are displayed as part of the 3D game, not as a stamp on your screen. You can use handles to put blue drag orbs around a brick, and you can change the color by changing the Color property. You can also switch them to Movement handles by editing the Style.

ARCHANDLES

These are similar to Handles but have an orbit-like circle around the axis.

SELECTIONBOX

This mimics the box around a brick when you select it. It's almost the same except that you can change the color. You can choose the brick it appears on in the same way that you set Handles and ArcHandles.

SELECTIONPARTLASSO

This has two properties for setting where it appears, which are Humanoid and Part. These are both object properties that have to be set like Adornee. If you set the Humanoid to play solo and the Part to any brick, then a line or lasso will appear from your torso and into the brick.

SELECTIONPOINTLASSO

This is similar to SelectionPartLasso except that it uses a Point instead of a Part. The Point is a Vector3 value and is the other end of the lasso.

SURFACESELECTION

This is similar to the SelectionBox but it selects a certain face of a brick. This can be edited in the Explorer panel.

ANOTHER PRACTICE GUI

Here's another practice GUI if you still aren't quite sure how to use them. First, right-click on StarterGUI, go to Insert Object, and then select ScreenGUI. Remember that ScreenGUI is basically a placeholder and won't have anything in it yet. Next, you can right-click on the ScreenGUI in the Explorer and insert an ImageLabel. Now you should see a picture in the top left corner of the screen.

This is a placeholder image, but you might want to add a custom image. Open the File menu and select Publish to Roblox As. Click ImageLabel in the Explorer, and in Properties find the property called Image. Click on the value and Add Image, which will let you choose an image from your computer. When you have selected an image, you will see it instead of the placeholder image you initially inserted. You can now reposition and resize it to make the image any size, at any place on the screen.

| FILE | | | | | HOME | MODEL | TERRAIN | TEST | VIEW | PLUGINS |

| Explorer | Properties | Start Page | Game Explorer | Toolbox | Context Help | Tutorials | Object Browser | Output | Script Analysis | Command Bar |

Show

Toolbox

Start Page × Baseplate

Castle   Chair   Loom

Armor   Barrel   Arched

Table   Royal Bed   Shack

Bushes   Large   Bed

Wheat   Dock   Mill

Background: ☐ White ☐ Black ☐ None

Run a command

Accessory	EchoSoundEffect	Script	Cut Ctrl+X
AlignOrientation	EqualizerSoundEffect	ScrollingFrame	Copy Ctrl+C
AlignPosition	Explosion	Seat	Paste Into Ctrl+Shift+V
Animation	Fire	Sky	Duplicate Ctrl+D
Attachment	FlangeSoundEffect	Smoke	Delete Del
BallSocketConstraint	Folder	Sound	Rename
BillboardGui	ForceField	SoundGroup	
BindableEvent	Frame	Sparkles	Group Ctrl+G
BindableFunction	HingeConstraint	SpawnLocation	Ungroup Ctrl+U
BlockMesh	Humanoid	SpecialMesh	Select Children
BloomEffect	ImageButton	SpotLight	Zoom to F
BlurEffect	ImageLabel	SpringConstraint	
BodyAngularVelocity	IntConstrainedValue	StringValue	Select Connections
BodyForce	IntValue	SunRaysEffect	Swap Attachments
BodyGyro	Keyframe	SurfaceGui	
BodyPosition	LocalScript	SurfaceLight	Insert Part
BodyThrust	MeshPart	Team	Insert Object
BodyVelocity	Model	TextBox	Insert from File...
BoolValue	ModuleScript	TextButton	
BrickColorValue	NumberValue	TextLabel	Save to File...
CFrameValue	ObjectValue	Texture	Save to Roblox...
ChorusSoundEffect	Part	Tool	Create new LinkedSource...
ClickDetector	ParticleEmitter	Torque	Publish as Plugin...
Color3Value	PitchShiftSoundEffect	TremoloSoundEffect	Export Selection...
ColorCorrectionEffect	PointLight	TrussPart	
CompressorSoundEffect	PrismaticConstraint	Vector3Value	Help
Configuration	RayValue	VehicleSeat	
CornerWedgePart	RemoteEvent	WedgePart	
CylinderMesh	RemoteFunction		
Decal	ReverbSoundEffect		
Dialog	RocketPropulsion		
DialogChoice	RodConstraint		
DistortionSoundEffect	RopeConstraint		
DoubleConstrainedValue	ScreenGui		

CHAPTER 26
Tips and Tricks and Online Resources

Part of the fun of Roblox is playing games and going on adventures. Some of the things you need to know when you jump into Roblox games include the following.

WHAT KIND OF GEAR ARE YOU USING?

Roblox players can create any kind of gear they want, but different gear is used in different worlds and games. This is usually up to the owner of the world or the creator of the game. Some of the different types of gear you might be using include ranged weapons, explosives, power-ups, musical instruments, and building tools.

GETTING TO YOUR GEAR

You can click the backpack button at the top left corner to access your gear. This will open a screen that shows you what's inside your backpack, depending on what you have acquired in the game. You can also organize the items in your backpack by pressing the backpack button.

USING HOTKEYS

You can assign your gear to hotkeys in the top left-hand corner of the screen. This will show you the numbers that are assigned to your gear and what you need to press to activate it. You can change these hotkeys by going to your backpack and dragging the gear to the hotkeys.

DON'T FORGET TO GET YOUR BADGES

We covered a variety of badge options in another chapter, but there are many others you can earn in the individual games. These badges let you show off how well you've played and how active you've been. It's recommended that you earn badges rather than acquire them through free badge places.

Although we've already covered most of the Roblox secrets to getting you started, there are still more tips and tricks that might help you get the most out of your playing and creating. Some that you might find helpful, as well as the best online resources to check out, include the following:

- If you jump off the ground and use your sword, you can glide. It's recommended that you try again if this doesn't work the first time.
- To glide down, get a jetpack and then destroy it using a hammer.
- Fuse weapons by going to a place that has swords, like Telamon, and get your two weapons ready.
- When creating or building, always save throughout and create a backup of your place in case Roblox Studio crashes.

- You can get a broken ninja mask by obtaining a Perfection Head or Round Head, and then wearing it with your ninja mask.
- You can use blocks to fly by sticking two tiny white blocks to the upper part of your legs and pressing up or down.
- Freeze the game by pressing CTRL and F1 while playing.
- Click on the copy and delete tools after clicking on a zombie to start a zombie riot.
- The keys Y, X, T, B, H, and F can control planes and helicopters.

HELPFUL TIPS FOR BUILDING AND CREATING

Other tips you should be aware of when you start building and creating in Roblox involve using hotkeys, studio settings, and lighting tricks. For instance, using the hotkeys that are already set up for you in Roblox Studio can make creating easier and faster. Use CTRL + L to change your movement or rotation orientation from the global axis to the local one. Also, hotkeys like CTRL + Shift + N, which changes your part's state to Negate, and CTRL + I, which lets you access advanced object fields quickly, can come in handy, especially once you've memorized them.

You can also become more efficient in Studio if you modify some of its settings. To get to the settings, first go to File at the top left and click Settings, and then in the panels, you can change the settings according to your preferences. You may want to change the camera movement speed or reduce your camera speed to move around more accurately. You might also want to change settings such as EditQualityLevel, which is under the tab Rendering. Although it's set to Automatic, this could mean a setting that's a lower quality based on your system. To get the most out of the effects that are offered, it's recommended that you change this setting to 12 or higher.

The last tip involves lighting tricks that can make your game look crisp and well-lit. Simply find the Lighting object in your Explorer window in Studio and then press CTRL + I to open Advanced Objects. Then, search Effects in the search box and you'll see lighting and audio effects. Choose from suggestions like BloomEffect to add a glow, BlurEffect to blur the background when the player is focused on the menu, and SunRaysEffect to apply sun rays, which can be ideal for bright summertime maps.

HELPFUL ONLINE RESOURCES

Roblox: https://www.youtube.com/user/roblox

Roblox Support: https://en.help.roblox.com/hc/en-us

Roblox Forum: https://forum.roblox.com/Fo-rum/ShowForum.aspx?ForumID=14

Scripting Helpers: https://scriptinghelpers.org/

Roblox University: http://wiki.roblox.com/index.php?title=Roblox_University

Twitch TV: https://www.twitch.tv/roblox

SallyGreenGamer: https://www.youtube.com/watch?v=TYnCQiNOL9E

As with any game on the Internet, you will run into problems from time to time. With Roblox, this could mean general Roblox issues, problems with the website, difficulties with chat, or even graphics problems. Plus, there could be challenges that vary depending on whether you're building and creating games or actually playing them. We've covered some of the easiest problems to get past as well as their solutions here.

BASIC PROBLEMS WITH ROBLOX

If you're having basic problems such as getting a "cannot find Roblox" message in your browser or instructions to install Roblox even though you've already installed it, the fix is usually simple. These types of issues often happen when temporary files are corrupted or damaged, when Roblox or another program is running during installation, or when a firewall is keeping Roblox from starting. Sometimes, Roblox files may become corrupted as well.

If you think this might be the case, you can usually try rebooting your computer first and then try to play. Believe it or not, this solves many Roblox and Roblox Studio problems.

If rebooting doesn't work, you can reset your computer's Internet options. Whether you use Internet Explorer, Chrome, or Firefox, resetting could be helpful. First, open your browser. If it's Internet Explorer, open the gear icon and go to Internet Options. Next, open the Advanced tab and press the Reset button. Close Internet Explorer and then reopen your Web browser.

If that doesn't work, you may need to clear your browser's temporary Internet files in case any corruption issues have taken place. You should also check your firewall to see if it's preventing you from accessing Roblox. Finally, you can reinstall Roblox and update Internet Explorer.

WEBSITE PROBLEMS

Sometimes you might encounter problems regarding the website itself, such as the website displaying incorrectly, certain pages not loading or displaying errors, buttons or links that won't let you click them, problems logging in, and many others. For most of these problems and other general website issues, you can usually do the following to get back on track.

Clear your temporary Internet files and cookies. Each browser has instructions online for doing this. Make sure you restart your computer afterward to see if your issue has been resolved.

Disable your browser's add-ons. These are also referred to as extensions or plugins, depending on your browser. Try to disable all of your add-ons to see if it resolves your issue, then, re-enable them one at a time until the issue starts again so you can pinpoint the exact problem.

Reset Internet Options for Windows. After resetting, close Internet Explorer and then go back into your browser of choice.

Update Internet Explorer. Make sure you're using the latest version of your browser.

LOGIN PROBLEMS

Sometimes problems are more specific and involve things like logging in and out. If you're having login problems, you should first check the solutions for general website problems. If those don't fix your login problem, you can also check to see if your computer's clock is accurate. For some reason, this can affect your ability to log in to your account. If you still can't log in, you may have to contact Roblox for assistance.

Another problem that occurs is when you are logged in to your account but still appear as a guest in games. If this happens, you should reboot your computer, reset your Internet options, and check your system clock to see if you can fix the problem.

PROBLEMS WITH GRAPHICS

The last problem involves graphics, which can really affect your game and your ability

to enjoy Roblox. This includes issues such as messages that claim your graphics card is too old, Roblox crashing during game play, and games that look strange, with odd textures and warped images.

Graphics issues typically happen if you don't have the latest version of DirectX on your computer, or if your graphics card isn't updated or supported by Roblox. For these problems, you should reset Roblox graphics by opening Roblox Studio, going to the File menu and clicking Settings, and then OK. Next, click Reset All Settings in the lower left of the window.

You should also test your DirectX package and, if necessary, update it. Other fixes could include lowering your display's color quality and upgrading your graphics card driver. To find out which graphics card Roblox is using, go to Roblox Studio, open the Studio Settings, and click Diagnostics. Scroll down to GfxCard and you'll see the list of graphics cards Roblox is currently using.

So far we've covered how to handle some of the most common issues you might encounter, but once in a while you might run into something more serious, like a bad advertisement, malware, or spyware. In such cases, you should check to make sure there isn't another program or website causing the issue. Also, check the extensions you're using. If it's a malware or spyware issue, it's possible that there's a service running in your computer's background, in which case you'll need to run an anti-malware program to get rid of it. Once it's removed, it's recommended that you delete your browser cookies, clear your cache, and restart your computer to prevent the problem from returning.

PROBLEMS ON MOBILE DEVICES

These types of issues don't usually occur on mobile devices, but if they do, it could be another app that's to blame. You're also more susceptible if your mobile device is rooted or jailbroken, which is often the case when bad ads or malware are involved. You can try mobile anti-malware to get rid of the problem, or you can factory-restore your device.

Whether the malware or bad ads are on your PC or your mobile device, you can report the problem to Roblox if it persists.

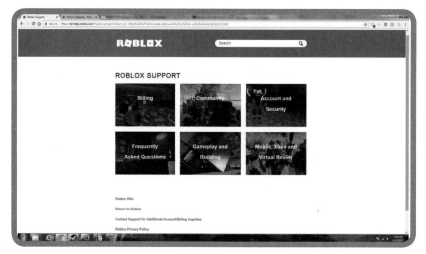

CHAPTER 28
Roblox Special Events

Roblox is always hosting special events for players to try new games and earn special prizes. One of the best-known events is the Roblox Easter Egg Hunt, which takes place each year and involves finding eggs across different worlds. Participants get a badge whenever they find an egg, and the egg corresponding to the badge will be a hat as well.

In 2017, the Easter Egg Hunt involved finding eggs to locate the mystery realm that holds the FabergEgg. If you found at least 40 eggs you could access the final realm, which would contain the final Fabergé Egg. There were also two bonus eggs that could be collected if players completed optional missions. The 2017 Egg Hunt broke the record, with nearly 40,000 players.

Some of the worlds in this game included the following.

STRATOSPHERE OUTPOST

This is where the Egg Hunt started. It was set in the Earth's atmosphere, with floating islands and a steampunk theme. There were five eggs here.

WORLD OF TOMORROW

This place was set in the future, with many technological advances. It included a metal tower, a large telescope, and even a rocket station. It also had mushrooms that glowed. There were seven eggs in this world.

NORTHERN ANTARCTICA

This was, of course, a frozen world set in the "north Antarctic," with a frozen lake, ski lodges, and a destroyed ship with a teleporter. This world had six eggs.

Other worlds that were part of the 2017 Egg Hunt were Arctic Battlegrounds, the Timeless Desert, Mount Ignis, Abyssal Plain, Shrine of the Eggs, and Stratosphere Settlement.

Besides being hidden in some of the most interesting worlds, the eggs that were hunted weren't too shabby either. These eggs weren't just ordinary eggs laid by chickens; they were sorted by location, each with an interesting name and background. For example, the Top of the World Egg was found on the top of the tower, which was the highest point in the map, and required players to touch it to acquire it. The World of Tomorrow had an egg called the Answer Egg, which was only obtainable every 450 minutes, or seven hours and 30 minutes, in real time. If the user visited Shallow Thought on time, the egg was awarded, but if the user was late they couldn't get the egg.

And then, of course, there were the Fabergé eggs. There was only one for the 2017 egg hunt, found at the Shrine of the Eggs, and it required 40 other eggs to obtain.

There was also special gear, such as the Roblox Egg Launcher, that Roblox Admin could use to spawn a Roblox egg in-game. It could only be used five times every two minutes and it launched a single Roblox egg. Another special item that was included was Bunny Ears. For a limited time, players could earn a boosted jump height and walkspeed for 75 percent off (25 Robux).

TIPS AND TRICKS FOR THE HUNT

Roblox events often include special tips and tricks to help you out from time to time as well. In the Egg Hunt, if you found two gray tubes, the tubes could spawn in different directions. A helpful hint was that you could determine an egg was fake by checking to see if it was moving. If it was moving, it was a lure, but if it wasn't moving, it was a real egg. You could also tell that an egg was fake if there was an anglerfish nearby.

As you can see, it's not only fun to create and play games with your friends and family members; you might have a blast participating in Roblox's big events like this one. If you missed this year's, make sure you keep your eyes and ears open for the next one.

ROBLOX TOURNAMENTS

Roblox also holds various tournaments you can join and has live-streamed them for years through its Twitch channel. Besides the events they normally host, they also plan to hold new challenges for players and developers through tournaments. For example, Roblox is currently looking for Roblox games that can be used in tournaments. Creators can submit their games for future tournaments, as long as they meet the following requirements:

- Filtering Enabled: Games will be featured on the Roblox Twitch stream, so filtering has to be enabled to ensure a game is safe and fun for all ages.
- Competitive: The games must be competitive and result in a metric that can be measured to determine a winner.
- Team Selection: The game has to be structured clearly as Team or Free For All play. For team play, the competitors must be able to select their team when they join the game.
- Game Length: The tournaments are limited in time to showcase games, and since they plan several rounds of multiple games, games should be able to be played quickly.
- Spectate Mode: Games must have the ability for noncompetitors to be in the game and view the action. The camera should be a third-person follow cam, the spectator should also be the game manager, and players should be able to join and choose to be competitors or spectators. Also, the spectator should have a GUI element to show which player is followed.

CHAPTER 29
Popular Roblox Games

Roblox games are constantly changing, with new ones being added every day. The most popular games will change over and over again. And you never know – it could be your game that ends up at the top of this list next time.

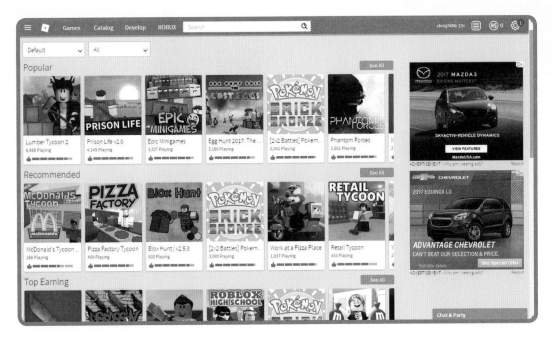

If you're looking for some games to try out, these are currently the most popular.

Prison Life v2.0

Epic Mini Games

Assassin!

MeepCity

Counter-Blox: Roblox Offensive

RoCitizens

Super Hero Tycoon

New School! Robloxian Life

Speed Run4

Dinosaur Simulator

Condo City Life

Miner's Haven

Theme Park Tycoon 2

Arcane Adventures

Apple Store Tycoon

Lumber Tycoon 2

Epic Mini Games

 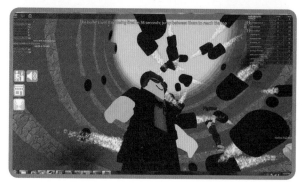

Murder Mystery 2

Phantom Forces

Roblox High School

Work at a Pizza Place

Whatever Floats Your Boat

Natural Disaster Survival

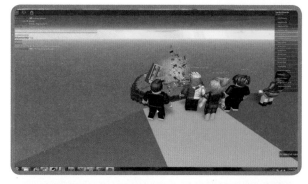

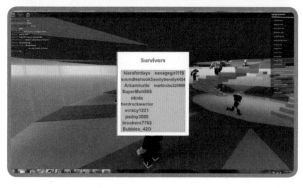

Bird Simulator

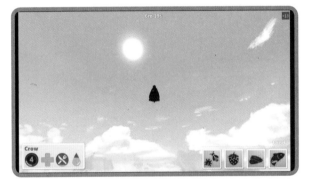

Pokémon Brick Bronze

Neighborhood of Robloxia

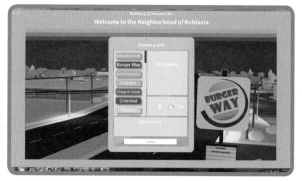

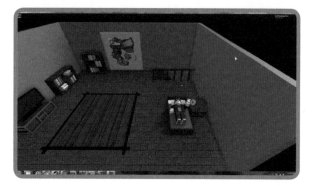

Red VS Blue VS Green VS Yellow

Vehicle Simulator

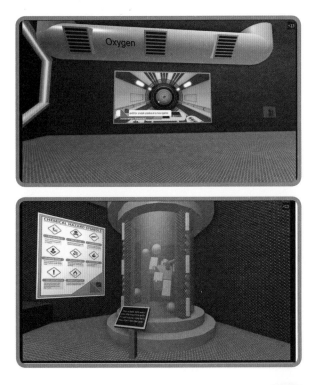

Game Space Travel